Virginia W

Edward de Vere, Seventeenth Earl of Oxford,
aged thirty-six. The St. Albans Portrait by Marcus
Gheeraedts, in the collection of the Duke of St.
Albans, a lineal descendant of Lord Oxford.

*Reproduced by courtesy of the Duke of St. Albans.
Photographed by the National Portrait Gallery.*

OXFORD,

Courtier To The Queen

A Biography By

ELEANOR BREWSTER

Pageant Press, Inc.   New York

To the Coxes and Bissells

I grapple them unto my soul
with hoops of steel.

ACKNOWLEDGMENTS

So many people have helped me in this biography that it is impossible to name them all; I can only send them silent thanks.

The original impetus for the study was sparked by *Shake-speare, The Man Behind The Name,* by Dorothy and Charlton Ogburn, Jr., William Morrow and Company. I have quoted also, as noted in the text, from *This Star of England,* by Dorothy and Charlton Ogburn, Coward McCann. I owe a debt of gratitude to all three Ogburns.

My thanks go to the Clarendon Press, Oxford; the Yale University Press; Harcourt, Brace and Company; and the Pageant Press for permission to quote from their books as noted; and to the Shakespeare Authorship Society, London, for timely help.

I am especially grateful to the Duke of St. Albans, and to the Duke of Portland for allowing me to reproduce portraits of the Earl of Oxford in their possession, and to use the Bolebec Crest. I wish to thank the Duke of Buccleuch; Mr. Simon Wingfield Digby, M.P.; and the National Portrait Gallery for permission to reproduce paintings in their collections; and to the British Museum for letting me reproduce the drawing of Queen Elizabeth, the engraving of the Queen and Lord Oxford, and the lines from *Sir Thomas More;* and to the New York Public Library for the prints of the Bolebec Crest and the engraving of Queen Elizabeth in the 1590's.

I am particularly grateful to the British Museum for

allowing me to do research in its treasure house, and to the Library of Trinity College, Hartford, for making it possible for me to study further.

And finally my deep thanks are due to Professor Morse Allen, formerly Chairman of the English Department, Trinity College, for his challenging criticism of my ms. as well as his encouragement, despite his disagreement with my viewpoint; and to my friend, Anne Dalton, without whose protective care it could never have been written.

E. B.

Hartford, Connecticut.

TABLE OF CONTENTS

Acknowledgment   **vi**

List of Illustrations   **ix**

Introduction   1

   I   Castle Hedingham   7

  II   Education   11

 III   Courtier to the Queen   25

 IV   Marriage   **35**

  V   Treachery   **42**

 VI   Return to Court   **48**

VII   Ann Vavasor   52

VIII   Return to Anne Cecil   **60**

 IX   The Players   71

  X   Poet and Playwright   75

 XI   Edward De Vere II   81

XII   Southampton   89

XIII   Elizabeth Trentham   100

XIV   Burghley   **109**

XV	The Queen: 1600	121
XVI	The Trial of Essex and Southampton	128
XVII	Last Years of the Queen and Her Courtier	140
XVIII	The Sonnets and Plays	149
XIX	The Portraits	161
	Bibliography	189
	Index	193

LIST OF ILLUSTRATIONS

Edward de Vere, Seventeenth Earl of Oxford: Frontispiece
By courtesy of the Duke of St. Albans

The Bolebec Crest: On title page and on the jacket
By courtesy of the Duke of St. Albans and the Duke of Portland

The following are grouped in a separate section after page 188.

William Cecil, First Baron Burghley
By courtesy of the National Portrait Gallery

Edward de Vere, Earl of Oxford
By courtesy of the Duke of Portland

Queen Elizabeth, 1575
By courtesy of the British Museum

Lord Burghley Presiding at the Court of Wards and Liveries, 1585
By courtesy of the Trustees of the Goodwood Collection

Lines from the play, *Sir Thomas More*
By courtesy of the British Museum

Henry Wriothesley, Third Earl of Southampton, in the Tower
By courtesy of the Duke of Portland and the National Portrait Gallery

Lord Oxford Carrying the Sword of State Before the Queen
By courtesy of the British Museum
Queen Elizabeth in Procession
By courtesy of Simon Wingfield Digby, M.P.
Queen Elizabeth in the late 1590's
By courtesy of the New York Public Library

Black and white were the Queen's personal colors, worn by the Earl of Oxford as her champion in the Royal Tilt Yard.

INTRODUCTION

In presenting this brief biography of Edward de Vere, seventeenth Earl of Oxford, a very large assumption is asked of the reader: namely, that he accept the premise that Lord Oxford is the true author of Shakespeare's plays and poetry. Volume upon volume has been written pro and con upon the theory that the actor from Stratford-on-Avon did not write the plays or poems ascribed to his name. Suffice it here to offer but one argument against the Stratford man, excellent though he may have been as an actor. If he really were the intellectual he must have been to write the plays, how does it happen that in his will, although he bequeaths valuable real estate, gold rings and a bedstead, he leaves not a single book? Moreover, in the wills of his two daughters and his granddaughter no mention is made of a folio of plays of the great dramatist, or even of a quarto. Indeed, not one of them bequeathed a single book! And this was in the early Stuart age when books were becoming commonplace. We

1

have records of other men and women of the Age of Elizabeth and the Age of James, which prove that anyone who even pretended to literary distinction left a library of books to his heirs. Why, even Elder William Brewster emigrating to the wilderness of the New World only four years after the death of Shakespeare, in 1620, brought over more than two hundred books on the Mayflower!

Granted that the actor was not the true author of the timeless plays, the next step was to narrow down the claimants to that honor. Bacon, Marlowe, Derby at one time or another have been suggested. The case for the Earl of Oxford was not seriously considered until the late J. T. Looney published a small volume in 1920, *Shakespeare Identified*. From those of us who believe that he happened upon the true author, Looney deserves eternal thanks.

Looney began his research with no preconceived idea who the true author might be. After studying the plays most carefully, he was able to make a list of general characteristics of the dramatist, such as:

A mature man of recognized genius.
Of intense sensibility.
Unconventional.
Of pronounced and known literary tastes.
An enthusiast in the world of drama.
A lyric poet of recognised talent.
Of superior education—classical—the habitual associate of educated people.
A member of the higher aristocracy.
Connected with Lancastrian supporters.
An enthusiast for Italy.
A follower of sport, including falconry.
A lover of music.
Doubtful and somewhat conflicting in his attitude to women.

2

Looney then proceeded to seek out the Elizabethan who best fitted the description. Only one possessed all the attributes he had listed: the Earl of Oxford.

Looney then compared the poems signed by the Earl with those we have come to know as Shakespeare's, and there he found striking similarities. Again, he re-read the plays in the light of the known facts of Oxford's life. The similarities were too numerous to be coincidental.

As an example of comedy, let us take one of the early plays, *All's Well That Ends Well*. This comedy is obviously written for a sophisticated, upper-class audience and indicates that the author had a sure familiarity with Court manners and mores. Here is the story: Bertram, a young noble of proud and ancient lineage, loses his father whom he loved and is brought up as a royal ward. Upon attaining manhood, he tries for military service and asks for permission to travel, but permission for both is refused. So he runs away soon after a forced marriage with a young woman with whom he has been brought up. So far the story exactly parallels the story of the life of Oxford.

Then take the play of *Hamlet*. Most critics agree that it contains autobiographic elements. The question then posed is, whose biography? Surely the story accords with the life of Oxford more closely than with the life of the Stratford man. Like Hamlet, Oxford dearly loved his father, who died. Like Hamlet's mother, Oxford's mother promptly married a former lover, deeply wounding her son with her indecent haste. Hamlet has a bosom friend, Horatio. Oxford had a close cousin, Sir Horace de Vere, a famous soldier in the War in the Low Countries. The dramatis personae include *Francisco, a soldier*. Sir Francis de Vere, also a soldier in the Netherlands War, was a brother of Sir Horace. Oxford had reason to be grateful to him for befriending his son, Edward, and arranging for Edward's education at Leyden.

3

Polonius has been recognised even by scholars of the "orthodox school" as being a portrayal of Lord Burghley. Certainly his relations with Ophelia closely resemble the relation between Lord Burghley and his daughter, Anne, whose unhappy marriage to Oxford must have been due in large part to her father's domineering influence upon her. It is worth noting that it was not Hamlet's treatment of Ophelia that drove her insane, but the death of her father which she couldn't face.

With Oxford in mind it is tempting to follow through even some of the less important allusions in *Hamlet*, as, for instance, Hamlet's speech to Horatio about the laxity of respect on the part of the gentry and its effect on "the peasant." The words almost paraphrase Queen Elizabeth's own when she forbade a duel between Lord Oxford and Sir Philip Sidney after their tennis court quarrel. There is even a reference to "falling out at tennis," which the courtly audience would immediately compare with the well-publicized quarrel mentioned above.

There is rather fascinating evidence in the poetry of the plays, and more especially in the sonnets, pointing to the authorship of Oxford. The careful reader will remark how frequently the word *ever* appears, and often with accent on the second syllable. Witness the last two lines of Sonnet 19:

> Yet do thy worst, old Time; despite thy wrong,
> My love shall in my verse ever live young.

Oxford makes use of the device of playing on his name in a poem he signed, called *Anne Vavasor's Echo Song*.[1] We quote only four lines:

1. *Anne Vavasor's Echo Song* will be found in full in the last pages of this book.

4

O heavens! who was the first that bred in me this
   fever? Vere.
Who was the first that gave the wound whose fear
   I wear for ever? Vere.
What tyrant, Cupid, to my harm usurpt thy golden
   quiver? Vere.
What wight first caught this heart and can from
   bondage it deliver? Vere.

To return to the plays, the preface to one of the
early editions of *Troilus and Cressida* has particular significance in this respect, to quote the Ogburns:

> "A never writer to an ever reader. Newes," can be
> read as a double pun on "E. Ver" (a nE. Ver writer to
> an E.Ver reader) and also as meaning a writer who
> can never appear, a never-known writer, to a constant
> reader.[2]

The Elizabethans delighted in these contrived conceits.
Indeed, it is thought that if more of the internal evidence
in the poetry could be revealed, more light might be
thrown upon the author, who wrote: "Every word doth
almost tell my name." E VERE, again.

After he was twenty-six Oxford never signed another
poem. It was just about this time that Shakespeare's plays
began to appear.

It is not our intention here to suggest that Lord
Oxford was the sole author of these famous dramas. Even
the authorities of the orthodox school admit that Shakespeare had collaborators. It was an Elizabethan custom.
Our quest is for the Master who directed the collaborators,
who took those old, tattered, time-worn plots and cast
them with people we recognize as our neighbors, who

---

2. *Shakespeare, the Real Man Behind the Name,* by Dorothy
Ogburn and Charlton Ogburn, Jr.

wrote prose that reads like poetry and poetry that is pure music.

But long before the plays were even thought of, the mysteries surrounding these two Elizabethans began to merge. It is a matter of record that Edward de Vere, Seventeenth Earl of Oxford, was born at Castle Hedingham, April 23rd, 1550. It will be recalled that traditionally William Shakespeare of Stratford-on-Avon was also born on April 23rd, but in the year 1564. However, *this* date April 23rd, is a matter of conjecture only because the only record we have is that of his christening recorded in the parish register as April 26th, 1564.

The Earl of Oxford was the center of a group of the most brilliant and witty literary men of the day. Frequent visitors to his mansion on the Strand include Marlowe, Chapman, Peele and Churchyard, to name only a few. Lyly and Munday were his secretaries, and two of his sons-in-law were literary patrons. William Stanley, Lord Derby, in particular, was a close friend and companion, and later, a son-in-law. There is even a possibility that Mary, Countess of Pembroke, was also a member of this celebrated gathering.

Gentle Reader, have you followed the argument thus far? Are you shaken even a little in your faith in the Swan of Avon theory of authorship? We Americans always want our facts proven beyond a shadow of doubt. But listen to the Bard:

> Ah, what a dusty answer gets the soul,
> When hot for certainties in this our life.

Even if you do not agree with the viewpoint from which this biography is written, it is the hope of the writer that you may enjoy reading the poignant story of Edward de Vere, Earl of Oxford, courtier to the Queen.

Chapter I

CASTLE HEDINGHAM

"Summer's lease hath all too short a day."
Sonnet 18.

Castle Hedingham in the green countryside of Essex was all astir that summer of 1561. Not only were the cooks in the kitchen belowstairs laying in vast quantities of lamb, venison, grain, fruit and vegetables. But his Lordship, the Sixteenth Earl of Oxford, who proudly held title to the oldest earldom in all England, was having a stage built in the Great Hall upon which the company of actors he sponsored were to present their plays.

His distinguished guests included his sister, Frances Vere Howard, a poetess in her own right, whose first husband, the Earl of Surrey, had been the most famous English poet of his day; another sister who was married to Baron Sheffield, composer of music and sonnets; and the brother of the Countess of Oxford, Arthur Golding, who had recently published his verse translation of the *Metamorphoses* of Ovid, its first translation into English. All the family would be present for this most festive occasion.

Our interest centers around the Earl's young son, eleven-year-old Edward de Vere, Viscount Bolebec, who had been called home from Cambridge University where he had been a student at Queen's College since he was nine years old.

The reason for these preparations at Castle Hedingham was the impending five-day visit of the new Queen, Elizabeth. She was twenty-eight years old with a regal carriage that was to distinguish her all her life. She had sparkling gray-green eyes, golden hair and that fragile beauty of face inherited from her mother, Anne Boleyn. We know her portrait of this time, the peaches and cream complexion, the pointed chin, the beautifully shaped hands which, we are told, she used so expressively. Elizabeth was an intellectual, witty and quick at repartee. She would be in her element in the stimulating climate of this castle. It would be an interesting visit.

And what about Edward, heir to the ancient earldom; what kind of a boy was he? His portrait shows us a auburn haired aristocrat with rosy cheeks, a long nose, and almond-shaped, penetrating dark eyes. He is handsome in a sort of brooding way with a compelling personality even at this age. He is known to have been precocious mentally and endowed with a scholar's love of learning. He had a keen interest in drama, which was not surprising, since for seven years the actors maintained by his father returned every winter to Hedingham after summer in the provinces, to present plays for the entertainment of the Earl and his visitors. How could this boy help growing up with a love for play-acting!

It is unfortunate that no record of the Queen's visit to Hedingham has been preserved for us, no program by which we might follow the exciting events of each day as they happened. But if this visit were anything like other royal visits of which we do have record, we may imagine that the five days were filled with color and pageantry and that the expense of the lavish ceremonies would cost the host several years' income.

The Queen's entourage would be met at the county boundary and escorted by the host along the winding lanes between green meadows to the entrance gate of the Castle, its great Norman keep looming stark in the distance beyond the trees. The Queen herself, dressed in the latest fashion, would be riding a white palfrey, Lord Oxford on one side of her, Sir Robert Dudley, the current favorite, on the other, with Sir William Cecil, her Principal Secretary, riding an ambling nag not far behind. They would be followed by her pretty Maids of Honor all colorfully dressed, courtiers in gorgeous apparel, the retainers and baggage carts bringing up the rear of the long procession.

At the Castle gate there would be a flattering speech of welcome, acknowledged by the guest of honor in a graceful compliment to the host. There would be divine service in the Chapel in which the Almighty would be rendered thanks for allowing the Castle the honor of harboring the royal visitor. There would be learned conversations in the Library on philosophy, poetry and other subjects, in which the Queen, gesturing with her lovely hands, would exchange quips in Latin or French with her host and the invited guests. Elizabeth was justly proud of her learning and enjoyed the stimulation of other trained minds. There would be feasts of many courses in which the rarest delicacies of the countryside would be brought forth to tempt her appetite, washed down by imported wines, while soft music would be tinkling down from the Minstrel Gallery. The Queen herself would be persuaded to play upon the virginals, which she did exceeding well.

Later there would be deer hunting in the Park and exhibitions of falconry, perhaps even tilting in the Court-yard to display the prowess of the courtiers. There would be dancing, especially the new volta which the Queen enjoyed because Sir Robert would lift her high.

And there would be the plays for which Lord Oxford had ordered his Great Hall to be turned into a veritable theatre. Of all the entertainment this was the most pleasing to her Majesty for she loved play-acting, and the Earl of Oxford's Company were professional players well schooled by performances rehearsed to perfection in the country before daring to appear before the Queen.

Such was the setting for the first meeting of our two protagonists, Elizabeth Tudor, still young at twenty-eight, and Edward de Vere, the eleven-year-old boy—old beyond his years, sensitive, impressionable, unpredictable, even as the Queen herself.

It was a portentous meeting.

Note to Chapter I. Could it be more than a curious coincidence that an old inhabitant a few years ago, referring to Castle Hedingham, said: "There's a tradition in the village that Shakespeare wrote some of his plays in the castle."?

This incident reported by Dorothy Ogburn and Charlton Ogburn Jr. in *Shake-speare: the Man Behind the Name.*

Chapter II

EDUCATION

"Neither a borrower nor a lender be . . . ."
Polonius in *Hamlet.*

The year after the Queen's visit to Castle Hedingham, the Earl of Oxford died, leaving young Edward, his twelve-year-old son to become the Seventeenth Earl and hereditary Lord Great Chamberlain of the Realm. The de Veres, claiming descent from Charlemagne, had come over from the small French town of Ver with William the Conqueror, whose half-sister married Aubrey de Vere, founder of the family. The de Vere motto was *Vero nil Verius,* or *Vero nihil Veritas,*[1] as it is sometimes written, "Nothing is truer than truth." Their emblem was a silver star.

However, to the young boy, Edward, these honors must have seemed a heavy responsibility in that fateful

1. Burke's *Peerage.*

year, 1562. It was a year of tragic changes for him, and hardest of all was the loss of his father, for he and the Sixteenth Earl had been very close.

Edward was forced to leave Castle Hedingham, the ancestral home he so loved, and to become a Royal Ward under the guardianship of Sir William Cecil, Secretary to the Queen. Sir William took the boy into his own great mansion, Cecil House on the Strand, in London. The abrupt change from country to city was another adjustment for the youthful nobleman to make, and though Cecil House was outside the limits of the City of London, the Strand must nevertheless have seemed to him muddy, crowded and noisy after the quiet countryside he had known. A contemporary complains that "carts and coaches make such a thundering as if the world ran upon wheels."

We have a description of young Edward's somber arrival, riding at the head of one hundred and forty retainers, all dressed in heavy black.

The next few years of his life he spent in Cecil House, which stood about where the Hotel Cecil is now. Here the unhappy little boy pursued his education with the distinguished tutors chosen for him by his guardian.

To live in the household of Sir William Cecil was in itself something of an education. Sir William possessed an ordered mind and showed an avid curiosity about everything that came to his attention, especially when it concerned England. However, his chief characteristic was his unruffled calm spirit.

We have a description of Cecil House as it was when Edward came there to live. It was, we are told, "a fayer house standing on the North side of the Strande, raysed with bricks proportionably adorned with four turrets," [2]

---

2. *Burghley,* by Rev. William Henry Charlton, Stamford, England. 1847.

on the four corners of the house. It was "curiously bewti-
fied within with rare devises, and especially by the oratory
placed in the angle of the great chamber." Moreover, it
contained the finest library and the finest private collection of books in London.

The mansion had originally belonged to St. Martin's
in the Fields, but Cecil had added to the monastic build-
ing and greatly improved its appearance. It had a famous
garden which, with its surrounding field, occupied the
land up to and including what is now Covent Garden.
Not only its garden was famous, but also the gardener,
Gerard, who was noted for his cultivation of herbs in
his own small plot on High Holborn and for his develop-
ment of roses for the garden of Sir William. Indeed, many
of the roses we know today were first cultivated by Gerard
in the garden of Cecil House.

The plays have many references to roses, as:

> What's in a name? that which we call a rose
> By any other name would smell as sweet.
> > *Romeo and Juliet.*
>
> But earthly happier is the rose distill'd,
> Grows, lives, and dies, in single blessedness.
> > *Midsummer Night's Dream*
>
> He wears the rose
> Of youth upon him.
> > *Antony and Cleopatra.*

King Richard II was called "the Rose King." And of
course, we are reminded immediately of the famous scene
described in *King Henry VI* (Pt. I, Act. II, sc. 4) in which
Somerset plucks a red rose for Lancaster and Warwick
a white rose for York, beginning the War of the Roses.
Edward must have known and loved gardener Gerard's
roses.

Sir William Cecil kept eighty persons as retainers in his London residence, their wages amounting to thirty pounds a week when the Cecils were not in residence, and upward of forty when they were. The Secretary lived in the style befitting his exalted station, the expenses of his table alone amounting to over one thousand marks a year. The Secretary also had a retinue of some twenty young gentlemen of noble birth in attendance, and English aristocrats were eager to have their young sons in his service.

Sir William was particularly genial at meal times; indeed, an invitation to dine at Cecil House was a coveted honor. The Queen

> "did sup with me even before the houe was quite finished,

Sir William noted in his diary.

Among the frequent guests at Cecil House and at Theobalds, one of Sir William's country estates, was Lady Lennox, mother of Lord Darnley; hence, she was mother-in-law to Mary Queen of Scots. This old lady took a particular fancy to Edward de Vere, Burghley's ward, and we have at least one record of their being at Theobalds together and of her interest in the charming young earl. This is significant because the author of *Macbeth* has copied a passage from the *Buik of Croniclis of Scotland* almost word for word. This history was in manuscript and circulated *only* among members of the royal family of Scotland. Therefore, Lady Lennox was the only person in England who could have owned a copy.[3]

Both Sir William and his illustrious but formidable wife, the Lady Mildred Cecil, were intellectuals, and it

---

3. See Profesor Louis P. Benezet, *The Six Loves of "Shake-speare."*

is certain from existing letters that each of them was sincerely fond of the young ward, Edward de Vere. Sir William could appreciate his fine intellect and seems most anxious to give the boy the best possible education. The Cecil children—Thomas; Robert, the little hunchback; Anne; and Elizabeth—were somewhat younger than Edward. However, they and the other noblemen's sons could have made Cecil House a pleasant place for a boy to grow up.

But apparently it wasn't. Edward was a lonely little fellow, mourning his father's death, and bitterly resenting anyone who attempted to fill his place. As always when he was unhappy, he sought consolation in his studies, which at this time included Latin, French, cosmography, writing, drawing and music, while his leisure was spent in "commendable exercise," like riding, shooting and dancing. There is today a letter written at this time by Edward to his guardian in beautiful French.

The young student was fortunate indeed in the tutors chosen for him: his uncle, Arthur Golding; Sir Thomas Smith; and Laurence Nowell, brother of the Dean of St. Paul's.

Arthur Golding had recently published his verse translation of Ovid's *Metamorphoses,* from which Edward quoted frequently, and which he seemed to know well and to enjoy.

Sir Thomas Smith had been a classmate of Cecil at Cambridge. He became a noted lawyer who was to have a lasting and beneficial influence on English law. Among other suggestions for correcting existing abuses, he wrote that putting pressure on a jury was "accounted very violent, tyrannical and contrary to the liberty and customs of the realm of England." He insisted that the liberty of the meanest subject was something precious, an inalienable possession of the Englishman.[4] How very *English* that sounds! And what a fascinating man for Edward to study under!

Edward's third tutor was Laurence Nowell, perhaps the most interesting of the three. Nowell is regarded as the chief reviver of the Anglo-Saxon language and learning. In the Bodleian Library, Oxford, there is a manuscript of an Old English dictionary that he wrote.[5] Nowell had an intense curiosity to learn every aspect of the land of Britain. In 1563 he made a proposal to Sir William Cecil for help in making maps of the entire country and all its separate shires. Only a few exquisitely finished maps of his remain to us, but one of them seems to have been carried about by Sir William with notations in his own hand. Nowell's map of Scotland is said to be "in advance of that of the great Mercator." [6]

Nowell also made transcripts from the Venerable Bede, Giraldus Cambrensis and Matthew Paris. He wrote a description of Ireland which, unfortunately, is now lost. He also attempted to classify and codify the laws of the Anglo-Saxons. But he never published any of his work.

We find young Edward de Vere serving at Court almost as soon as he came to London, though we cannot ascertain whether, as a Royal Ward, he would have started his career as a page, or as a courtier. Since he was the Premier Earl of the Realm, as well as hereditary Great Chamberlain, it is assumed that even at this early age he served as courtier to the Queen.

It was in this difficult period in any young man's life that Edward's sorrows came, like Hamlet's, "not single spies but in battalions." The first came while he was still

4. A. L. Rowse, *The England of Elizabeth.*
5. Ibid.
6. Rowse, op. cit.

grieving intensely over his father's death. In indecent
haste, only a few weeks after the funeral, his mother married a former suitor, Sir Charles Tyrrel. Edward bitterly
resented his mother's marriage, and after this she seems to
have dropped quite out of his life.

Do we not recognize this open wound in Hamlet's sar-
castic retort to Horatio, who has told him he came home
"to see your father's funeral."

"I think," remarks the prince, "it was to see my
mother's marriage."

"Indeed, my Lord," replies Horatio, "it followed hard
upon." And then comes Hamlet's famous line:

"Thrift, thrift, Horatio. The funeral baked meats did
coldly furnish forth the marriage tables."

But soon after this another blow fell upon the bent
head of this unhappy youth. His sister, Baroness Windsor,
claimed that his father and mother had never been married and that therefore the estates should come to her.
The claim was utterly false, but gossip spread, wounding
to the quick the pride of the youthful earl. And most dis-
turbing of all, the Queen delighted in taunting him by
asking in front of all the Court, "How's our young bastard
this morning?" Edward was heard to grumble that "the
Queen sayd he was a bastard for whiche cause he wold
never love hir, and wold leave hir in the lurche one day."
Later he changed his mind, but he never quite forgave
her this insult. He worked out his resentment in a poem,
The Loss of My Good Name, the first poem we know to
which he signed his name:

> Fram'd in the front of forlorn hope past all recovery
> I stayless stand to abide the shock of shame and infamy.
> My life, though ling'ring long, is lodg'd in lair of
>   loathsome ways;
> My death delay'd to keep from life the harm of hapless
>   days.

My sprites, my heart, my wit and force, in deep distres
   are drown'd;
The only loss of my good name is of these griefs the
   ground.
And since my mind, my wit, my head, my voice and
   tongue are weak,
To utter, move, devise, conceive, sound forth, declare
   and speak
Such piercing plaints as answer might, or would my
   woeful case;
Help crave I must, and crave I will, with tears upon
   my face,
To wail with me this loss of mine, as of these griefs
   the ground.
Help God, help saints, help sprites and powers that in
   heaven do dwell,
Help man, help beasts, help birds and worms, that on
   the earth do toil,
Help fish, help fowl, that flock and feed upon the salt
   sea soil,
Help echo that in air doth flee, shrill voices to resound,
To wail this loss of my good name, as of these griefs
   the ground.

                                                        E. O.

What a young man's poem this is, with its repetition of
figures of speech! The use of alliteration Edward might
have picked up from his studies of Anglo-Saxon literature
with Nowell, while the phrase, "in earth do dwell" seems
to have been suggested by Arthur Golding's translation of
the *Metamorphoses*: "or in the heaven do dwell." [7]

In June of 1563 Laurence Nowell asked the Secretary
to find him other work, as his services to the young Lord
Oxford "were no longer required." Nowell later became
Dean of Lichfield Cathedral, while his young scholar went

---

7. Golding's Translation of Ovid's *Metamorphoses*, VII, 326.

on to be one of the brightest stars in the firmament in those spacious days of Queen Elizabeth.

Edward de Vere went back to Cambridge, only this time instead of returning to Queen's College, he went to St. John's. This had been Sir William's college, and doubtless it was through his guardian's influence that Edward became a student there. The Secretary was at this time Chancellor of the University.

Although noblemen in those days entered the university at an early age, Edward seems to have been even younger than most, due to his fine tutoring and his own exceptionally brilliant mind. It was the custom for each student to be under the care of an older private tutor, who would stand to him *in loco parentis,* be a companion, see to his expenditures, and help him with his studies. Instruction was in Latin, and the curriculum included rhetoric, mathematics and medicine, the text books for the latter being Galen and Hippocrates. The academic study of music was rare, but since Edward showed such marked talent for it, he certainly would have included music, too. A nobleman was granted a Bachelor of Arts degree in less than the seven years prescribed for ordinary scholars—usually in about four years.

By the time of Queen Elizabeth, life for students in the university had become more comfortable than it had been previously. A nobleman might find himself well housed, with glass in his chamber windows, panelled walls to his rooms, and hangings of painted cloth. He could have shelves put in for his books, rushes for the floor, a chest for his linen and clothing, and the luxury of a feather bed to sleep under. And he could have one of the "poor scholars" waken him in the morning in time for chapel, clean his boots, and run his errands.

Meals were served in the college dining hall, earls and

barons sitting at the Fellows' Table, which, of course, was more plentifully and expensively served than those of the second table that accommodated the Master of Arts students, gentlemen and eminent citizens, while the third table, for "people of low condition," got what was left. Eleven a.m. was the hour for dinner, and supper was served at five in the afternoon. During the meal a student would read aloud from the Bible, and after grace had been rendered at the end, the student was free to retire to his own chambers.

Discipline was strict, at least for commoners. A typical punishment was to be "scanted of sizes," meaning to be deprived of the allowance of bread and drink from the buttery, and students found in inns and taverns were punished by public flogging.

Statutes of individual colleges reflect the customs of the times. One forbids undergraduates "to encourage an inordinate growth of hair" under penalty of a fourpenny fine. Another forbids "singing, making a noise, shouting, or discharging guns, or (making) any other kind of uproar or din" which might disturb students wishing to sleep or to study. And students were not allowed to walk abroad alone.

The authorities of Cambridge tried to cope with the outlandish attire of its fashionable undergraduate fops, but apparently without success. Silks, satins and "excessive ruffs" were frowned upon. And in this connection we might mention that it was while he was at St. John's that Edward incurred the wrath of his guardian for the first of his lifelong extravagances by overspending his wardrobe allowance!

Athletics at Cambridge consisted of football, archery and quoits, all of which were considered "legitimate games."

But undergraduate life was not all lectures, athletics and discipline. While plays in the vernacular were banned as being corrupters of youth, Latin plays were accepted as part of the curriculum. Hence, even a most virtuous scholar might perform in one without disgrace. Usually the plays were given on Saturday and Sunday evenings, and, provided it were in Latin, a student play might be produced as well as those of the classical playwrights.

We have reason to believe that it was while he was an undergraduate at Cambridge that Edward began to write plays, though what the plays were, and whether any of them were written in English, we do not know.

Plays and merrymaking reached their peak annually during the Christmas holiday, which lasted till Twelfth Night. Most students did not leave the university to go home. Discipline was relaxed for this period, and the time was given over to mummery and festivities. There would be a "Christmas Prince," or Lord of Misrule, who would preside over all programs during the holiday until studies were resumed in January. His role seems to have been to try to keep a semblance of order.

There were other special occasions, too. The year that Edward received his degree, the Queen paid a state visit to Cambridge, which included the usual formal addresses of welcome and parting, and in between a round of academic exercises, preachings and plays. That year in honor of the Queen there was a special presentation of *Aulularia* by Plautus.

Lord Bacon has drawn for us an uncomplimentary picture of the Elizabethan universities. Yet it is considered that, with all their faults and deficiencies, Oxford and Cambridge compared favorably with the most famous contemporary universities on the Continent. Together with the Court, the universities, as "the compendium of all

England," provided the training ground for public servants.

Such is a brief résumé of the curriculum and customs of Cambridge when Edward de Vere was a student. He won his Bachelor of Arts degree from his alma mater in 1564, at the age of fourteen and a half. Two years later Oxford University awarded him a Master of Arts. As a postgraduate student there he had been a member of Christ Church College, known to the nobility as "the House."

In 1567 we find Edward enrolled at Gray's Inn, where Sir William himself had received his training in the law. Being a little outside of London, in the open country, Gray's Inn was considered healthier than Lincoln's Inn, or the Middle or Inner Temple. Together these four Inns of Court comprised what was perhaps the finest legal university in Europe. Nevertheless, the students must have pursued other subjects there, also. Fortescue tells us:

> There is both in the Inns of Court and the Inns of Chancery a sort of academy or gymnasium fit for persons of their station, (the nobility) where they learn all kinds of music, dancing and other such accomplishments and diversions, which are called revels, as are suitable for their quality, and such as are usually practised at Court. At other times, out of term, the greater part apply themselves to the study of the law . . . So that knights, barons, and the greatest nobility of the kingdom often place their children in the Inns of Court, not so much to make the law their study, much less to live by the profession, having large patrimonies of their own, but to form their manners and to preserve them from the contagion of vice. The only way they have of punishing delin-

quents is by expelling them from the society, which punishment they dread more than criminals do imprisonment and irons.

Gray's Inn was especially noted for its famous graduates, among whom were Sir Nicholas Bacon, Lord Keeper of the Great Seal, as well as his illustrious brother-in-law, Sir William Cecil, Secretary to the Queen.

When Edward de Vere enrolled at Gray's Inn, he found these regulations in dress, among others, which were enforced with a fine:

(Students) are forbidden to wear on their doublets and hose any light colours, except scarlets and crimsons, nor wear any upper velvet cap, or any scarf or wings on their gown, white feathers or ribbons on their caps, upon pain to forfeit, for the first default, 3s.4d., and the second expulsion without redemption. . . .

The regulations proceeded to prohibit anyone under the degree of knight to wear any beard above three weeks' growth upon pain of 40s. fine. No hat to be worn in hall at dinner or supper time—fine, 3s.4d. No boots or spurs to be worn in hall, but members shall come with their academic caps "decently and orderly." There were also severe prohibitions against laundresses or other women servants under the age of forty years!

Meals in the dining hall consisted of bread and beer for breakfast; beef or mutton for dinner, and on Easter Day eggs and green sauce; bread and mugs of beer for supper.

Legal instruction was given in a method which was a combination of debate, tutorial classes and lectures, and during the season that the Law Courts were in session, members of the Inn were allowed to attend. Also, they were allowed to practice law as solicitors.

When Edward was at Gray's Inn, a fellow student was a young man from Penshurst, in Kent, named Philip Sidney. Unfortunately the two youths were not very congenial.

We have proof of the literary tastes of the young Earl of Oxford from the list of his expenditures in 1569-70, when he was nineteen. (And we surmise also that Cecil demanded not only that his spendthrift ward record his expenses, but that they were later meticulously examined by his guardian!) Here is the list: "Geneva bible, a Chaucer, Plutarch's Works in French, with other books and papers." And again: "Tully's and Plautus' works in folio."

After Gray's Inn, Edward de Vere had completed his formal education. He was now ready to give full time to being a courtier to the Queen.

Chapter III

COURTIER TO THE QUEEN

"For princes are the glass, the school, the book,
Where subjects' eyes do learn, do read, do look."
The Rape of Lucrece, Stanza 5.

The Queen held Court in one or another of her royal
residences more or less according to the season. By
Candlemas Day, February twelfth, it was time to move
into the country, to Greenwich, or Richmond, or even
to Hampton Court, though this was the palace she liked
least because she had been desperately sick with smallpox
there in 1562.

St. George's Day, April twenty-third, would find her
at Windsor Castle for the great Feast of the Knights of
the Order of the Garter. The knights to be created would
ride out to meet her with much ceremony and at great
expense to themselves.

25

July and August were months for royal pilgrimages and visits to the nobility, as at Castle Hedingham, where she had been the guest of the Sixteenth Earl of Oxford; or Kenilworth, where she had been the guest of her favorite, Sir Robert Dudley, now Earl of Leicester. The Queen loved these imposed visitations and undoubtedly they increased her popularity with the people. But her coming was a mixed blessing to her hosts, for a royal visit, as we have seen, meant the expense of lavish display and entertainment of the many Court attendants and retainers.

Always in November, with the tingle of winter in the air, the Queen turned toward London, where Parliament would be sitting and the Law Courts in session at Westminster. She planned to be at Whitehall for Accession Day, November seventeenth, which was celebrated all over the kingdom with bonfires on the hills, and at Court by "running at tilt," a combat on horseback with spears, which the Queen particularly liked to watch.

A royal transit between palaces was accomplished with great ceremony, sometimes by river, sometimes by road. A foreign ambassador was frequently invited, doubtless to be impressed by the adulation for the Queen along the way. Wherever she went, church bells would peal forth their chimes, and the people would stop their work and come out in great crowds to hail the royal procession as it went along.

Each journey was accompanied by a long train of baggage carts bearing the royal paraphernalia. Though the movements of the Court were expected with the seasons, the actual date of departure was determined by the whim of the Lady Sovereign, and she frequently changed her mind. There is a story of the head carter, having packed and unpacked five times, waiting in the courtyard for the signal to go—when a voice from an upper window ordered him to delay once more.

"Begad!" he was heard to mutter audibly. "The Queen is no different from my wife!"

Whitehall was a great conglomeration of buildings with no coherent plan. Like Hampton Court, it had been built by Cardinal Wolsey, and Elizabeth's father had made it convenient for the cardinal to present it as a gift to the Crown. The Palace covered some scores of acres between Westminster and Charing Cross, and through its midst ran the highway to the City of London. To the west of the highway lay the Tilt Yard, Cockpit, and many lodgings whose mullioned windows faced St. James' Park. To the east were the Privy Garden, the Royal Chapel and the Apartments of State extending almost down to the river bank. Beyond them, toward Charing Cross, was the Fruit Orchard, while across the river on the Surrey side, the Royal Barge was moored. Sumptuously appointed, and drawn by a boatful of rowers, the barge was a frequent sight on the Thames during the months when the Queen was in residence.

This was the arrangement of rooms inside the palace: the Great Hall, of course, was its center with a raised dais from which a door led into the Guard, or Watching Chamber. Out of this a door opened into the Presence Chamber. From there one entered the Privy Chamber, which gave access to the Queen's Private Apartments.

The Presence Chamber and the Privy Chamber were essential elements of the scheme, and no matter where the Queen might choose to stay, this arrangement of rooms had to be contrived.

Courtiers awaiting the pleasure of the Queen would

gather in the Presence Chamber and play cards or backgammon until summoned to attend her. It was a large room, hung with rich tapestries; the floor covered with rushes, or "hay." [1]

It is here in the Presence Chamber that our young hero, the Earl of Oxford, must have spent a great deal of his time when first he came to Court, waiting—waiting for the summons that would bring him to her Majesty for some ceremonial service, or perhaps only that she might enjoy his charming companionship and beguiling conversation. Meanwhile, Edward de Vere would be kept waiting, waiting, one of the few pastimes at which he did not excel. Did he play cards with the other courtiers, probably the younger ones, like his classmate, Philip Sidney? Perhaps. It is also likely that we might find him in animated conversation with one of the older noblemen, like his father's friend, the Earl of Sussex. Or perhaps he might be planning a masque or a new play to be performed at Christmas.

He is not in the Presence Chamber on the particular Sunday morning we have chosen to visit Court to see the Queen on her way to Chapel, although we shall recognize him shortly in her train.

The great chamber is full of people—indeed, anybody allowed into the palace at all is entitled to come here, perhaps to present a petition to her Majesty, perhaps in the hope of being noticed by her, perhaps only to gaze upon her, "our Sovereign Lady, Queen Elizabeth," prayed for in the Litany every Sunday in church. This particular

---

1. "Suppose the singing birds musicians;
    The grass whereon thou thread'st, the presence strew'd."
                                    King Richard II, Act 1, sc. 3.

Sunday morning the Archbishop of Canterbury is here talking with the Bishop of London, each of them in his black satin robes of state with white linen rochet. They are standing a little apart from the crowd, and before the Queen approaches, they precede her to the Chapel to prepare for divine service.

As the time draws near, all eyes are on the closed door of the dais, guarded by a gentleman in velvet wearing a heavy gold chain. At last he opens the door, having received the knock from within, and the procession emerges.[2]

Leading the courtiers are the gentlemen of lowest rank, followed by the barons and earls and Knights of the Garter, all richly dressed and bareheaded.

Next comes the Lord Chancellor with the Seals of State in a red silk purse. On one side of him is the Earl of Shrewsbury, carrying the Royal Sceptre. On the other side we see our handsome hero, the youthful Earl of Oxford, bearing the Sword of State in its red scabbard studded with golden fleurs-de-lis, the point of the sword turned upward.

And now comes the Queen herself, very stately and majestic in a gorgeous white silk gown "embroidered with pearls the size of peas." She wears a necklace of gold and many jewels, and her gown is low-cut as is the custom for unmarried ladies. She is neither tall nor short but very regal, and she seems to be speaking softly to those around her, gesturing with her beautiful hands as she speaks. Her gown has a long heavy train, which is borne by one of her noble Lady Attendants. Behind her are her Maids of Honor, most of them dressed in white, and all "very

---

2. Most of this description is taken from E. K. Chambers' chapter on "The Court," in *Shakespeare's England*, Vol. I.

handsome and well-shaped." The Queen and the Maids of Honor are guarded on each side by fifty gentlemen pensioners with gilt battle-axes.

As the Queen moves along, the people fall on their knees like a field of wheat before a summer breeze. Now and again she will raise a kneeling person with her hand, now speak graciously to one, now to another, her voice and manner "mild and obliging." She turns easily from French to Latin, "Scotch or Dutch," depending on the nationality of the person favored. And whoever speaks to her, if not already kneeling, drops on one knee.

Now a petition is presented to her, which she graciously receives, and this is the occasion for acclamation of "Long live Queen Elizabeth!" which she answers graciously with "I thank you, my good people!"

And so she slowly passes on to Chapel.

A German visitor describes for us what happens in the Presence Chamber before the midday meal.[3] The royal dinner is brought in by yeomen of the guard "clothed in scarlet with a golden rose on their backs," to the "music" of drums and trumpets. This service is done with great solemnity, after which a countess rubs each plate with bread and salt and gives a morsel of each dish to a guard to taste. Then the dishes are removed to the Privy Chamber by the Queen's Ladies.

Sometimes Queen Elizabeth would eat dinner in public in the Great Hall, a custom of the early English kings which she revived. She would be served by her principal noblemen on bended knee, and we may be sure that this was one of the duties of the handsome Earl of Oxford.

The Presence Chamber was, as we have said, open to

---

3. Ibid.

anybody who was allowed to come to Court, but access to the Privy Chamber was jealously guarded. Here the Queen would pass the time of day with her ladies and whomever else she might choose to have shown in, perhaps an ambassador, or her Secretary, or more likely, her current favorite.

To anyone loving dramatics as much as Edward did, the Court of Queen Elizabeth must have been a thrilling place to be in the late 1560's. As we have seen, the Queen herself loved a good show, loved to see one and even more to be the center of it. She delighted in impromptu and spectacular torchlight processions through the dark streets of London, attended by her gay young courtiers.

When she opened Parliament she was carried to Westminster Palace in a litter, wearing a red velvet cloak, a golden crown on her golden hair, while her Maids of Honor rode in single file behind her. We have a painting of Edward, aged twenty-three, walking beside the Queen's litter, carrying the Sword of State. There is also an engraving of the Queen opening Parliament at about this time. On her right is Lord Burghley; on her left, Walsingham, Secretary of State. In front of Burghley stands the Earl of Shrewsbury, Earl Marshal of the Kingdom, while in front of Walsingham stands the Earl of Oxford, the Lord Great Chamberlain, again bearing the Sword of State.

Besides waiting, and attending the Queen on ceremonial occasions, Edward must have spent his days in the Tilt Yard and on the Royal Tennis Court, while evenings doubtless he would dance the galliard, step a pavane, or tread a measure of a coranto. When he wasn't dancing, he might be tossing off a graceful poem to a lady, or composing an air for her to play on the virginals. Edward excelled in all of these, and we learn from a contemporary writing in the year 1567 that he was the darling of the inner circle at Court, nicknamed "Phoebus," referring to the Greek god, Phoebus Apollo.[4]

No wonder the Queen, all her life susceptible to attractive young men, should single him out for her favors. By this time the Earl of Leicester was aging, and here was a gallant young nobleman right at her feet whose person and conversation were more congenial to her. How far this infatuation went may never be known. Yet it must be acknowledged that Queen Elizabeth, though beautiful and scholarly, was at heart a very coarse woman—a side of her character which fortunately she showed only in private. How could she be otherwise, being the daughter of Henry VIII? Meanwhile, Edward could hardly defend himself from the attentions showered upon him by his Liege Sovereign.

We have external evidence pointing to Elizabeth's more than platonic interest in her young courtier. The son of the Earl of Shrewsbury writes to his father in 1572 of the Earl of Oxford:

> The Queen's Majesty delighteth more in his personage, and in his dancing and his valiantness than any other. If it were not for his fickle head he would pass any of them (i.e., the courtiers) shortly. . . . At all these love matters my Lord Burghley winketh, and will not meddle in any way.

---

4. Giles Fletcher wrote this tribute to Lord Oxford's horsemanship: "He controls his foaming steed with a light rein, and armed with a long spear rides to the encounter. Fearlessly he settles himself in the saddle, gracefully bending his body this way and that. Now he circles round; now with spurred heel he rouses his charger. The gallant animal with fiery energy collects himself, and flying quicker than the wind beats the ground with his hoofs, and again is pulled up short as the reins control him."

Another contemporary, unnamed, reports that the Queen "wooed the Earl of Oxford" when he was a young courtier.

Even Mary Queen of Scots wrote a letter to her royal cousin in which she referred to the Earl of Oxford as "being your lover."

Once in one of her flirtatious moods, Elizabeth sent a ring to the Duc d'Alençon, brother of the French King, during the period when negotiations were in process for her marriage to him. But after the Duke came to England and she met him and saw how extremely unattractive he was, she said:

"I would be shamed to lead a man no older than our own Oxford to the church," pretending that the years between them had been the bar to her marriage to the Earl.

Was Edward himself emotionally involved in his relations with the Queen? It would not be unlikely that the lonely, harassed young man, flattered at first, might well have fallen under the spell of this still fascinating and all-powerful woman with whom he had so much in common. They would have had much to talk about with one another, and how their conversation would have glittered with wit and repartee!

Yet this was an unnatural relationship, the Queen being seventeen years older than her urbane favorite. And though difference in age never stopped Elizabeth Tudor from flirting with a personable young man, we have evidence that this had been an unpleasant and distasteful experience to her courtier. Witness *Venus and Adonis!*

But though Elizabeth the woman might dally with a royal favorite, she knew well that if ever she did marry, the consort would have to be even more than heir to the oldest earldom in England. Indeed, there is a pathetic little poem by the Queen on this subject which gives us an insight into Elizabeth the woman—a very different creature from the imperious majesty to which we are accustomed. Here is the poem:

By Queen Elizabeth

I grieve; and dare not show my discontent!
  I love; and yet am forced to seem to hate!
I do; yet dare not say, I ever meant!
  I seem stark mute; but inwardly do prate!
    I am, and am not; I freeze, and yet am burned;
    Since from myself my other self I turned.

My care is like my shadow in the sun,
  Follows me flying! flies, when I pursue it!
Stands and lies by me! do'th what I have done!
  This too familiar CARE doth make me rue it!
    No means I find, to rid him from my breast,
    Till, by the end of things, it be supprest.

Some gentler Passions slide into my mind;
  For I am soft, and made of melting snow.
Or be more cruel, LOVE! and so be kind:
  Let me, or float, or sink! be high or low,
    Or let me live with some more sweet content;
    Or die! and so forget what LOVE e'er meant.[5]

We have evidence that the affair with the Queen left a lasting scar upon the personality of Edward de Vere. Long afterwards, recounting in Sonnet number 66 the afflictions which had plagued his youth, he writes of

. . . gilded honour shamefully misplac'd,
And maiden virtue rudely strumpeted . . .

5. From *The Spenser Anthology*, edited by Edward Alber, London, 1901.

34

Chapter IV

MARRIAGE

". . . to you a true and humble wife,
At all times to your will conformable."
King Henry VIII.

It was not long before Edward cooled in his affection for the Queen, if ever he had felt any real warmth toward her. He was tired of the hollow ceremonies of Court life and impatient with the endless hours of waiting. One evening in his cups he was heard to mumble that the Queen "had the worst voice and did everything with the worst grace that ever woman did!" Let us hope the indiscreet remark was not repeated to her Majesty! But Edward was beyond caring; he longed to stretch his wings, to see for himself the exciting world he had read so much about.

There is a contemporary story that Oxford, while kneeling before the Queen one day, "let out a fart." He was so embarrassed that he fled from the country. Much later when he returned, we can perhaps sense his blushing shame his first day at Court when his Sovereign greeted him with:

"My Lord, we had forgot the fart!"

Whether or not the "fart" story is true, we do know that there were other reasons why Edward wanted to leave England at this time.

The first reason was the impending prospect of his marriage to Anne Cecil, daughter of his guardian, the former Sir William, now Lord Burghley. Anne was five years younger than he, a quiet, lovable girl, but hardly one to attract his sophisticated tastes. Also he must have known her in Lord Burghley's house as a young sister ever since he was twelve years old, and romance seldom thrives on close acquaintance. Sir Henry Sidney had made several attempts to arrange a marriage between Anne and his young son, Philip. But Anne's wily father was aiming for higher stakes. Having recently won a coveted title for himself, what could better further his ambitions with the Queen than to marry Anne to the proudest Earl of the Realm, that is, provided that the Queen would relinquish him herself! Burghley must have sensed that she was ready to do so by this time, for the courtiers, too, were beginning to realize that any consort for their royal mistress would have to be of royal blood.

Moreover, Burghley had become genuinely fond of his young ward, as had everyone else who came within the range of his magnetic personality. "I confess to your Lordship," writes Burghley to the Earl of Rutland in regard to Oxford, "I do honour him so dearly from my heart as I do my own son, and in any case that may touch him for his honour and weal, I shall think him mine own interest therein. And surely, my Lord, by dealing with him, I find that which I often heard of your Lordship, there is much more in him of understanding than any stranger to him would think. And for my part, I find that whereof I take comfort in his wit and knowledge, grown by good observation." If only Lord Burghley could have kept this love and respect for his son-in-law!

The wedding was planned to take place at Theobalds. But alas! The bridegroom had run away to the Continent. He didn't get very far, as he invariably spent more money than he could afford, so it was not hard to find him and bring him home.

A second time the wedding was planned and this time Lord Burghley was taking no chances. The Queen herself was invited to be a witness. So we have the record of Mistress Anne Cecil marrying the young Earl of Oxford in Westminster Abbey in the presence of Queen Elizabeth, December 19, 1571. Anne, like Juliet, was in her fourteenth year. She is always described as "little Anne," "sweet," and "gentle" even as Juliet.

The wedding was a festive occasion. Lord St. John wrote to Oxford's cousin, the Earl of Rutland mentioned above: "The Earl (of Oxford) hath gotten him a wife—or at least a wife hath gotten him; whereto the Queen hath given her consent," and then he adds slyly, "while all the Maids of Honour mourned."

For one month the newlyweds seemed to be living happily together at Wivenhoe, Oxford's estate near Colchester. Then the troubles that ever beset this proud young earl began anew. His cousin, the Duke of Norfolk, aspired to marry Mary, the young and beautiful Queen of Scots, who, like himself, was a Catholic. There was even a plot among the Catholic faction to arrange that Mary and Norfolk supplant Queen Elizabeth on the throne of England. The plot, however, was discovered, and the Queen promptly imprisoned Norfolk in the Tower.

Edward tried in every way he could to have the sentence commuted, appealing first to his father-in-law, and then directly to the Queen. Failing to move either of them, he impulsively plotted to break into the Tower and rescue his cousin. The plot was foiled, and Edward, to nobody's surprise, was let off with a royal tongue-lashing. Five months later the Duke of Norfolk was beheaded on Tower Hill.

Next, Edward volunteered for fighting against the Spanish in the dreary little war dragging out in the Low Countries. He had for a short time served on the staff of his father's friend, the Earl of Sussex, in the Border War against the Scots. But neither the Queen nor his father-in-law were ready to forgive his implication in the Norfolk affair, and permission to leave England was not forthcoming.

As was his custom, Edward sought to drown his disappointment in literature. Bartholomew Clarke, his former professor at Cambridge, asked him to write a Latin introduction to Clarke's translation of Castiglione's *The Perfect Courtier*. Later Gabriel Harvey referred to this introduction in an address to Oxford and Cambridge Universities in the presence of the Queen and Court.

"Let this courtly epistle," he said, "more polished than the writings of Castiglione himself, witness how greatly thou dost excel in letters." Harvey further urged the young earl to put aside his pen and use his talents as a leader in defense of England against her enemies, using the phrase: *Vultus tela vibrat*—"Thy countenance shakes spears."

The Earls of Oxford also bore the title Viscount Bolebec, whose crest showed a lion brandishing a broken spear. It has been pointed out that the phrase *vultus tela vibrat* was undoubtedly a pun on the pen name *already* adopted by Edward. In further proof, let us note that after punning on the name, "Cecil," Harvey calls Burghley "Polus" three times. It is generally accepted that Polonius in *Hamlet* is a caricature of Burghley. An eminent Shakespeare scholar suggests that "we have here the earliest record of the pen name, *Shakespeare*," and also perhaps a clue to some nickname of Burghley—something that sounded like "Polus" or "Polonius."

While Edward was still cooling his heels in London, eager to be off to travel, he wrote a preface, including a poem, to his friend, Thomas Bedingfield's, translation into English of Cardanus' *Comfort*, even paying for its publication himself. This book, *Comfort*, has been known as *Hamlet's book*, since it embodies much of the philosophy of the melancholy Dane. This is Edward's poem:

Labour and its Reward

The Earl of Oxford to the Reader of Bedingfield's translation of Cardanus' *Comfort*.

The labouring man that tills the fertile soil,
   And reaps the harvest fruits, hath not indeed
The gain but pain; and if for all his toil
   He gets the straw, the lord will have the seed.

The manchet fine falls not unto his share;
   On coarsest cheat his hungry stomach feeds;
The landlord doth possess the finest fare;
   He pulls the flowers, he plucks but the weeds.

The mason poor that builds the lordly halls,
   Dwells not in them; they are for high degree;
His cottage is compact in paper walls,
   And not with brick or stone, as others be.

The idle drone that labours not at all,
    Sucks up the sweet of honey from the bee;
Who workest most to their share least doth fall,
    With due desert reward will never be.

The swiftest hare unto the mastive slow
    Oft-times doth fall, to him as for a prey;
The greyhound thereby doth miss his game we know
    For which he made such speedy haste away.

So he that takes the pain to pen the book,
    Reaps not the gifts of goodly golden muse;
But those gain that, who on the work shall look,
    And from the sour the sweet by skill shall choose;
For he that beats the bush the bird not gets,
But who sits still and holdeth fast the nets.

In the first five verses do we see the influence of Sir
Thomas Smith? Or is it perhaps Edward's innate sympathy
with people of every degree that enables him to write
so feelingly of the laboring man? This is a characteristic
we find in many of the plays.

Gilbert Talbot, that garrulous son of Bess of Hard-
wick, describes a play written by Edward and performed
at Court about this time. Would that Talbot had hinted
more broadly to let us know which play that was!

Edward was then living most of the time in bachelor
apartments at the Savoy, not only to be near Whitehall
in case he should be summoned hastily, but it was neces-
sary for him to have a place in London where he could
invite his literary friends. Many of these men of letters
were more bibulously inclined than the chaste young
Countess cared to entertain.

But while Edward was consorting with these learned
friends, it is no surprise to us to learn that Anne, so eager

to please her dashing husband, should write to the Lord Chamberlain in charge of arrangements at Hampton Court to allow three chambers instead of two, at a forthcoming visit there, "for the more commodious my lodging is, the willinger I hope the lord my husband will be to come thither." Poor little Anne! She was soon to learn that all her effort to hold her errant husband would be in vain. We find him fled to the Low Countries with Lord Seymour. In Brussels they were welcomed by the Earl of Westmoreland, banished from the English Court five years before for political reasons. Although accepting Westmoreland's hospitality, Edward himself never wavered in his loyalty to the Queen.

Meanwhile at the English Court there was a right royal rage at the disappearance of the favorite quite without royal permission. The Queen dispatched Thomas Bedingfield to bring him home, hardly assuaged in her wrath by the entreaties of the good old Earl of Sussex and Lord Burghley on behalf of the runaway. In a fortnight he was back in the fold, having been met at the paquet-boat by his father-in-law.

Again the Queen forgave Edward his desertion. What a way he had with him, this twenty-four-year-old nobleman! For on his importunings, Queen Elizabeth granted him permission for an extended trip abroad.

Chapter V.

TREACHERY

He is compos'd and fram'd of treachery."
Much Ado About Nothing.

This time Edward was away eighteen months, travelling with a retinue of nine men as befitting to his station. Lord Burghley noted the retinue in his diary: "two gentlemen, two grooms, one payend, a harbinger, a housekeeper and a trenchman." He went first to France, and from Paris the English Ambassador wrote back to Burghley:

> I presented my Lord of Oxford also to the King and Queen, who used him honourably. Amongst other talk the King asked whether he was married. I said he had a fair lady. "Il y a donc ce," said the king, "un beau couple."

While Edward was in Paris he received a note from Lord Burghley, his father-in-law, announcing the news of Anne's pregnancy and urging him to come home for the birth of his child. Oxford replied characteristically that, since soon there would be an heir to carry on the name of de Vere, he thought he'd better take this opportunity to go to see Italy.

However, Edward showed his concern for his expectant wife by sending her his portrait by a Flemish artist, and a pair of fine horses. We believe the portrait he sent is that known as the Welbeck.

On the way he visited the Rector of Strasbourg University. This learned scholar, Johann Sturm, entertained the young English courtier for five days, later writing to Lord Burghley that he never would forget the Lord Oxford and his remarkable command of Latin.

Crossing the Alps, Edward rode on into Venice where he found a warm welcome from the Italian noblemen alerted to his coming by the Venetian Ambassador to London. He also visited Padua, Mantua, Verona, Milan, Siena, Rome, Genoa and Palermo in Sicily, where he challenged "all manner of persons whatsoever, and at all manner of weapons, as Tournaments, Barriers, with horse and armour, to fight a combat with any whatsoever in defence of his Prince and Country. For which he was very highly commended, and yet no man durst be so hardy to encounter with him." At the end of the tour he was speaking Italian like a native. He was later known in England as "the Italianate nobleman," a term somewhat derogatory, though a compliment also.

By chance we have a remarkably vivid description of the Earl of Oxford on this tour, in a speech in one of Chapman's plays, *The Revenge of Bussy d'Amboise,* the picture, a tribute from one leading dramatist to another:

I overtook, coming from Italy,
In Germany, a great and famous Earl

Of England: the most goodly fashion'd man
I ever saw; from head to foot in form
Rare and most absolute; he had a face
Like one of the most ancient honour'd Romans,
From whence his noblest family was deriv'd;
He was beside of spirit passing great,
Valiant, and learn'd, and liberal as the sun,
Spoke and writ sweetly or of learned subjects,
Or of the discipline of public weals;
And 'twas the Earl of Oxford.

We can sense the growing hostility between Lord
Oxford and his father-in-law in the letters Edward wrote
to him from the Continent appealing for more funds for
his travels. Here is part of one of those letters:

My Lord, whereas I perceive by your Lordship's letters
how hardly money is to be gotten, and that my man
writeth he would fain pay unto my creditors some part
of that money which I have appointed to be made over
unto me; good my Lord, let rather my creditors bear
with me awhile, and take their days assured according
to that order I left, than I so want in a strange
country, unknowing yet what need I may have of
money myself. My revenue is appointed, with the
profits of my lands, to pay them as I may; and if I
cannot yet pay them as I would, yet as I can I will,
but preferring my own necessity before theirs . . .

Another time he wrote to Burghley, apparently in
answer to a rebuke:

Whereas I understand the greatness of my debt and
greediness of my creditors grows so dishonourable and
troublesome to your Lordship, that that land of mine
which is in Cornwall I have appointed to be sold.

But again tragedy—indeed, treachery—was to join his company. Edward was tired of travel now and joyfully anticipating his return to England, when the blow fell. Lord Howard, his cousin, and brother to the beheaded Duke of Norfolk, seems to have had a machiavellian cunning in sowing dissension and discord wherever he went. He spread gossip at Court that Edward was not the father of Anne's child. As though the gentle and devoted Anne *could* have been unfaithful to him! But the dastardly lie would not be downed, and the whole Court waited with fiendish glee to see how Oxford would greet his wife on homecoming.

Not content to let this horrid news drift across the Channel, Lord Howard went so far as to meet Edward and his retinue in Paris to tell him the report. Poor Edward, ready at last to settle down to the warmth and comfort of his own hearth, to embrace his wife and to see his new babe! And now this heartbreaking news completely overturned his domestic life.

Whether 'tis nobler in the mind
To suffer the slings and arrows of outrageous fortune,
Or to take arms against a sea of troubles,
And by opposing end them.

Edward decided to oppose them, though his sea of troubles by no means came to an end. He embarked for England. On the way, as though he hadn't enough troubles already, his ship was attacked by pirates, to whom he lost some valuable possessions.

Anne and her father were at the pier to meet his ship, but he stalked by them without a greeting and went straight to the Queen. He refused to live with his wife, forbade her even to come to Court. Lord Burghley never forgave his son-in-law the humiliation and sorrow he inflicted upon poor Anne. At first Burghley tried to reason with Edward, begging him not to believe "liars and malicious backbiters." Edward did not reply to that letter and the coolness between them worsened. Soon Edward realized that he was being spied upon. There is a letter today from Burghley to Anne urging *her* to spy upon her husband if ever he should come home to live.

Do we not recognise the anguish and frustration of the unhappy courtier in Sonnet 121:

> 'Tis better to be vile than vile esteem'd,
> When not to be receives reproach of being;
> And just pleasure lost, which is so deem'd
> Not by our feeling, but by other's seeing;
> . . . .
> No, I am that I am, and they that level
> At my abuses reckon up their own;
> I may be straight though they themselves be bevel;
> By their rank thoughts my deeds must not be shown; . . .

Note the phrase from the Geneva Bible, which we know Edward had bought when he was nineteen: "I am that I am."

At the same time Edward wrote the following letter to his father-in-law, in which he uses the same phrase again:

> My Lord, this other day your man, Stainner, told me that you sent for Amis, my man, and if he were absent, that Lyly [1] should come unto you. I sent Amis,

---

1. "Lyly" mentioned in this letter was Oxford's secretary, John Lyly, 1553-1606, author of *Eupheues, or The Anatomy of Wit*. Between 1584 and 1585 he wrote plays for the Children of the Chapel Royal and the Children of St. Paul's.

for he was in the way. And I think it very strange that your Lordship should enter into that course toward me; whereby I must learn that (which) I new not before, both of your opinion and good will toward me; But I pray, my Lord, leave that course, for I mean not to be your ward nor your child. I serve her Majesty and I am that I am; by alliance near to your lordship, but free; and scorn to be offered that injury to think that I am so weak of government as to be ruled by servants, or not able to govern myself.

Again we may pity Anne Cecil. Her husband was soon to console himself with another by her name.

Chapter VI.

RETURN TO COURT

"How weary, stale, flat, and unprofitable seem to
me the uses of this world."

Hamlet.

Upon his return to England Edward flung himself
with renewed zest into the familiar routine of Court life
that he had run away from only eighteen months before.
There is reason to believe that her Majesty welcomed him
home with more than queenly warmth. He had brought
her a present from Italy, "a paire of perfumed Gloves [1]
trimmed only with foure Tuftes of roses of colored silks,"
which pleased her so much that she had her portrait

---

1. Stow writes that it was after this that gloves and girdles
embroidered with silk and gold thread began to be stocked in the
London shops.

painted in them.[2] How she must have revelled in the tall tales he told about his travels! Perhaps she was ready to resume the dalliance with this mercurial young earl, separated irreparably, it would seem, from his lawful wife. It was at this time that Mary Queen of Scots wrote to her cousin Elizabeth that "the Earl of Oxford dared not become reconciled to his wife for fear of losing the favor that he enjoys through being your lover." That shows how far the gossip had spread.

It might be noted here that in 1577 the Queen bestowed a parcel of land worth £250 on "our faithful cousin, the Earl of Oxford," and we know that the Queen seldom gave away anything without expecting something in return.

But though the Court of Queen Elizabeth might gossip and chatter about its own small affairs, yet the minds and imaginations of these noblemen and noblewomen, and of the Queen herself, were stretched and quickened by news of the explorers' voyages and discoveries in the New World. Exciting stories of Indians and "Eskimaux," and most enticing of all, stories of gold, flooded the Court, and new maps were drawn and redrawn as new knowledge became available.

It is not surprising to find that in 1578 Edward de Vere took out shares in Martin Frobisher's Third Expedition. He had wanted to accompany the explorer himself, but

---

2. Consider three references to gloves in the plays:

The gloves the Count sent me; they are an excellent perfume.
    Much Ado About Nothing. Act III, sc. 4.
Give me your gloves, I'll wear them for your sake.
    Merchant of Venice. Act IV, sc. 1.
Gloves as sweet as damask roses.
    Winter's Tale, Act IV, cs. 4.

since this seemed to be impossible, he made the lavish investment of several thousand pounds. Sir Philip Sidney contributed only £167.10s, and his sister, the Countess of Pembroke, £33.15s. Oxford was always prodigal with money, especially when the project fired his imagination.

But despite the excitement of coming home to England and the festivities of the London season at Court, Edward was inwardly aching and miserable which he showed outwardly by being fractious and sulky.

One day he had a quarrel on the royal tennis court with that "perfect knight," Sir Philip Sidney. During the altercation he infuriated Sidney by calling him: "Puppy!"

Sidney drew himself up and said with asperity:

"Dogs beget puppies. Men beget children," and promptly challenged Edward to a duel. But the Queen heard about it, and doubtless though she secretly relished the fracas, forbade the duel, pointing out "the difference in degrees owed to superiors, and how the Gentleman's neglect of the Nobility taught the peasant to insult both." The Sidney family, though noble, was considerably inferior to the de Veres in the accepted social scale of those days.

It is perhaps worth comparing Hamlet's remark:

"By the Lord, Horatio . . . the age is grown so picked that the toe of the peasant comes so near the heel of the courtier he galls his kibe."

Again, in *Hamlet,* we note that Polonius instructs his man to spy upon Laertes, mentioning a "falling out at tennis" as an example of the "slight sullies" he discovers in his son.

There never had been much love lost between Edward and Sir Philip Sidney. In Spenser's *Anthology of Poetry* [3]

---

3. Both poems are from *The Spenser Anthology,* edited by Edward Alber, London, 1901.

we find two poems that must have been exchanged at either before or after the tennis court quarrel. This is Edward's, which seems to have fallen into the hands of Sidney:

Were I a King, I might command content!
    Were I obscure, unknown should be my cares!
And were I dead; no thoughts should me torment,
        No words, nor wrongs, nor love, nor hate, nor fears!
            A doubtful choice for me, these three things to
            crave!
            A Kingdom! or a Cottage! or a Grave!

This is Sir Philip's answer:

Wert thou a King, yet not command content;
    Since empire none, thy mind could yet suffice!
Wert thou obscure! still cares would thee torment!
    But wert thou dead; all care and sorrow dies!
        An easy choice, of three things, one to crave,
        No Kingdom, nor a Cottage; but a Grave!

Edward in his desperate and unhappy state turned to his Catholic cousins, the Howards, for solace and consolation. He became secretly converted to the Catholic faith, a rather dangerous turnabout for a de Vere in those precarious days. Later, when the Queen heard that he was going to Mass, she forced him to renounce the old religion and to be a good Protestant as his father had been. Edward refers to this in the revealing sonnet, number 66:

And purest faith unhappily forsworn.

This, then, was the mood and this the situation of our hero when Fate intervened and dealt him the most shattering experience of his life.

Chapter VII.

ANNE VAVASOR

"Love is a smoke made with the fumes of sighs;
Being purged, a fire sparkling in lovers' eyes;
Being vex'd, a sea nourish'd with loving tears:
What is it else? a madness."

Romeo and Juliet.

It was that evil genius, that Iago, Lord Henry Howard, who brought Anne Vavasor to Court, and whether he intentionally planned to entangle his cousin, Lord Oxford, in her coils, we shall never know. Anne was a distant cousin of Howard from the north country, whom he had sponsored to that finishing school for Elizabethan young ladies, a position of Maid of Honor to the Queen. She was just sixteen.

Anne Vavasor was the antithesis of Anne Cecil. She was clever, witty, and caustic; she loved the quick retort, she delighted in rapier-pointed repartee. She could write poetry, of a sort, which perhaps helped her to appreciate other poet's efforts. Among her host of admirers was

Edmund Spenser, who immortalized her as his "Rosalind."

We see her in her portrait, dark, proud and chic in her wheel farthingale, with deep starched lace ruff and a bee-hive hair-do. She was no beauty, this Anne, yet even in her portrait there is something of that sensual attraction that infatuated so many of the gentlemen of Queen Elizabeth's Court. Our poet has painted an even more vivid picture of her. He refers to her "mourning eyes," "lofty velvet brow," and skin unusually fine and smooth, "lac'd with blue of heaven's own tinct." She liked music —a sure bond!—and she was skilled at playing on the virginals. While watching her play, her lover would envy the "nimble jacks" which leapt from the wooden keyboard to kiss the "tender inward" of her playing fingers.

Edward fell desperately in love with her with all the fervor of his warm and passionate nature. Indeed, the vision of this Anne was to haunt him for most of the rest of his life. Many times he drew her picture for us in the plays, and we recognize her full-length presentation in Cleopatra—dark, bewitching and eternally seductive.

This was a love that comes only once in a lifetime, and for Edward it was an all-consuming experience. Sonnet 57 tells the extent of his passion:

> Being your slave, what should I do but tend
> Upon the hours and times of your desire?
> I have no precious time at all to spend,
> Nor services to do, till you require.
> Nor dare I chide the world-without-end hour
> Whilst I, my sovereign, watch the clock for you,
> Nor think the bitterness of absence sour
> When you have bid your servant once adieu;
> Nor dare I question with my jealous thought
> Where you may be, or your affairs suppose,
> But, like a sad slave, stay and think of nought,
> Save where you are how happy you make those.

Here he is again, waiting. But now how differently! When Edward waited for the Queen, he was bored; now he is tortured.

The next sonnet, number 58, again harps on his slavery to her whims, and is also a pun on her name, Vavasor, meaning Master of Vassals.

> That god forbid that made me first your slave,
> I should in thought control your times of pleasure,
> Or at your hand the account of hours crave,
> Being your vassal, bound to stay your leisure!

The hurt and anguish of his love are reflected in the sonnets, which, had not Anne been the strumpet that she was, might never have been wrenched from Edward's tormented soul. In them we follow the precarious progress of this tragic story.

The Queen, ever jealous of her young Maids in Waiting, this time had cause to be. There is a record of a tournament at Court in January, 1581, in which the Earl of Oxford was victor. Graciously the Queen herself bestowed on him the prize, a set of score cards or tallies, on which to record the results of games and tournaments—a handsome thing, bound in gold and studded with diamonds. This much we know. We further surmise that later Elizabeth Tudor's all-seeing eyes spotted the tallies in the possession of her minion, Anne! After the royal rage had subsided, the harassed lover wrote this sonnet to his Sovereign: (Sonnet 122.)

> Thy gifts, thy tables, are within my brain
> Full character'd with lasting memory,
> Which shall above that idle rank remain
> Beyond all date, even to eternity;
> Or at least, so long as brain and heart
> Have faculty by nature to subsist;

54

Till each to raz'd oblivion yield his part
Of thee, thy record never can be miss'd.
That poor retention could not so much hold,
Nor need I tallies thy dear love to score;
Therefore to give them from me was I bold
To trust those tables that receive thee more;
    To keep an adjunct to remember thee
    Were to import forgetfulness in me.

Not long after this episode, another plot to bring the Queen of Scots to the English throne became known, and though Oxford denounced his cousins, the Howards, they insisted that he had been their leader. The story of Edward's efforts to appease her Majesty and clear his own name is told in a letter of the French Ambassador to his king, in which he said that Oxford was "put to confusion in the presence of his Mistress," and that "he has lost credit and honour by all the ladies of the Court." Yet he must have had a strong hold over the Queen still, because she let him go free, although she sent his cousins to the Tower.

Here is his reflection on those trying days, in Sonnet 29:

When in disgrace with Fortune and men's eyes,
I all alone beweep my outcast state,
And trouble deaf heaven with my bootless cries
And look upon myself and curse my fate,
Wishing me like to one more rich in hope,
Featur'd like him, like him with friends possess'd,
Desiring this man's art, and that man's scope,
With what I most enjoy contented least;
Yet in these thoughts myself almost despising,
Haply I think on thee, and then my state,
Like to the lark at break of day arising
From sullen earth, sings hymns at heaven's gate;
    For thy sweet love remember'd such wealth brings
    That then I scorn to change my state with kings.

But further disgrace was to follow. A letter from Walsingham, dated March 23rd, 1581, tells that "Anne Vavysor was brought to bed of a son in the Maiden's Chamber. The E. of Oxford is avowed to be the father."

Edward tried to get away to the Continent, but all ports were closed to him. He was brought back to London and committed to the Tower, where Anne and her child were already imprisoned. Although the men and women prisoners were incarcerated in different parts of the Tower, it is likely that Anne and her lover met at some time or other, perhaps when they were allowed to take the air on the ramparts. And were there harsh words from her, deserted by her lover, left to face her shame alone? Perhaps. Sonnet 109 reads:

> O, never say that I was false of heart,
> Though absence seem'd my flame to qualify.
> As easy might I from myself depart
> As from my soul, which in thy breast doth lie.

Without squirming an inch, how eloquently Edward was able to pacify his ladies!

Upon release from prison, Anne did not return to Court, as she was no longer a "Maid of Honour." She went on to further conquests. She had several husbands, two of them at one time, and any number of lovers in between. Needless to say, she was faithful to none. Before she was twenty, she had borne two illegitimate sons, both of whom grew up to have distinguished careers. She lived to be over ninety, still alluring, we suppose, even in old age.

Anne Vavasor will appear in our story unexpectedly several times again, though never with that fresh appeal she had when she first came down to Court from the north country, when she was sixteen.

But be it said of Anne Vavasor that she kept Edward's young son with her and brought him up to be a pride and joy to his father, while he, in turn, gave the child his name, Edward de Vere.

Then worse misfortune awaited Edward's release from the Tower. Anne's uncle, Sir Thomas Knyvvet, not only challenged Edward to a duel, but set his retainers to fighting Oxford's men, too. Again we quote the French Ambassador writing home: "The streets of London were filled with the Quarrelling clamors of these Montagues and Capulets." Twice the Earl and Sir Thomas fought. In the second duel each combatant was seriously wounded, Edward being lamed for life. There are four references to the Author's lameness in the sonnets:

I, made lame by fortune's dearest spite. Sonnet 37.

Then I am not lame, poor nor despis'd. Sonnet 37.

Speak of my lameness, and I straight will halt. Sonnet 89.

And strength by limping sway disabled. Sonnet 66.

That Edward had been wracked with jealousy, that he suspected his best friend as his rival, that he tortured himself with ambivalent emotions of love and hate, we know only too well from the sonnets.

Who was the handsome youth who was his bitter rival? He could have been any number of courtiers with whom Anne flirted. Researchers of "the Oxford School" believe that it was Henry Wriothesley, Earl of Southampton. Comparisons of dates, however, proves this theory impossible, for in 1581, the year Anne Vavasor gave birth to Oxford's son, Southampton was only eight years old—hardly a formidable rival!

Here is one more of the many mysteries in the life of Edward de Vere. We quote Sonnet number 42, which he wrote at the time of his consuming jealousy:

That thou hast her, it is not all my grief,
And yet it may be said I loved her dearly;
That she hath thee, is of my wailing chief,
A loss in love that touches me more nearly.
Loving offenders, thus I will excuse ye:
Thou dost love her, because thou know'st I love her;
And for my sake even so doth she abuse me,
Suffering my friend for my sake to approve her.
If I love thee, my loss is my love's gain,
And losing her, my friend hath found that loss;
Both find each other, and I lose both twain,
And both for my sake lay on me this cross:
    But here's the joy; my friend and I are one;
    Sweet flattery! then she loves me but alone.

Although the love of Anne Vavasor was the great passion of Edward's life, yet break with her he did, though never irreparably. Perhaps their common fate in the Tower had something to do with hastening their separation upon release. In Sonnet 137 we find Edward cursing his folly in falling for her.

Thou blind fool, Love, what dost thou to mine eyes,
That they behold, and see not what they see?
They know what beauty is, see where it lies,
Yet what the best is take the worst to be.
If eyes, corrupt by over-partial looks,
Be anchor'd in the bay where all men ride,
Why of eyes' falsehood hast thou forged hooks,
Whereto the judgment of my heart is tied?
Why should my heart think that a several plot

Which my heart knows the wide world's common place?
Or mine eyes, seeing this, say this is not,
To put fair truth upon so foul a face?
    In things right true my heart and eyes have err'd,
    And to this false plague are they now transferr'd.

Note here again the reference to *truth,* and remember the family motto: *Nothing is truer than truth.*

Edward was not only disillusioned by Anne Vavasor. He was also thoroughly fed up with Court life and in the grip of profound melancholy. Sonnet 66 tells the story:

Tir'd with all these, for restful death I cry
As to behold desert a beggar born,
And needy nothing trimm'd in jollity,
And purest faith unhappily forsworn,
And gilded honour shamefully misplac'd,
And maiden virtue rudely strumpeted,
And right perfection wrongfully disgrac'd,
And strength by limping sway disabled,
And art made tongue-tied by authority,
And folly—doctor-like—controlling skill,
And simple truth miscall'd simplicity,
And captive good attending captain ill:
    Tir'd with all these, from these would I be gone,
    Save that to die, I leave my love alone.

Who is "my love" this time? We have evidence that it is Anne Cecil, who has been loving him all these years.

Note to Chapter VII: For suggestions relating individual sonnets to episodes in the life of the Earl of Oxford I am indebted to Professor Louis P. Benezet and his book, *The Six Loves of "Shakespeare."*

Chapter VIII

RETURN TO ANNE CECIL

"Now prove
Our loving lawful, and our faith not torn."
Love's Labour's Lost.

When life was at its lowest ebb, Edward received this
letter from his estranged wife, Anne:

My Lord, In what misery I may account myself to
be, that neither can see any end thereof nor yet any
hope to diminish it. And now of late having had some
hope in my own conceit that your Lordship would
have renewed some part of your favour that you
began to show me this summer, though you seemed
fearful that you began it by open address. Now after
long silence of hearing nothing from you, at the
length I am informed—but how truly I know not,
and yet how uncomfortably I do not seek it—that your
Lordship is entered into some misliking of me with-

out any cause in deed or thought. And therefore, my
good Lord, I beseech you in the name of that God
which knoweth all my thoughts and love towards
you, let me know the cause you are moved to continue me in this misery, and what you would have me
to do in my power to recover your constant favour,
so as your Lordship may not be led still to detain me
in calamity without some probable cause, whereof,
I appeal to God, I am utterly innocent.

Edward's reply may well have been Sonnet 117:

> Accuse me thus: that I have scanted all
> Wherein I should your great deserts repay,
> Forgot upon your dearest love to call,
> Whereto all bonds do tie me day by day:
> That I have frequent been with unknown minds,
> And given to time your own dear-purchased right:
> That I have hoisted sail to all the winds
> Which should transport me farthest from your sight.
> Book both my wilfulnes and errors down,
> And on just proof surmise accumulate;
> Bring me within the level of your frown,
> But shoot not at me in your waken'd hate;
>   Since my appeal says I did strive to prove
>   The constancy and virtue of your love.

And Sonnet number 118, which is even more revealing:

> Like as, to make our appetites more keen,
> With eager compounds we our palate urge,
> As, to prevent our maladies unseen,
> We sicken to shun sickness when we purge;
> Even so, being full of your ne'er cloying sweetness,
> To bitter sauces did I frame my feeding;
> And, sick of welfare, found a kind of meetness

To be diseased, ere, that there was true needing.
Thus policy in love, to anticipate
The ills that were not, grew to faults assur'd,
And brought to medicine a healthful state,
Which, rank of goodness, would by ill be cur'd;
    But thence I learn, and find the lesson true,
    Drugs poison him that so fell sick of you.

Edward and Anne were reconciled. Edward was still young and charming, thirty-two in 1582, and Anne was a forgiving wife. Her reward was Sonnet 119:

What portions have I drunk of Siren tears,
Distill'd from limbecks foul as hell within,
Applying fears to hopes, and hopes to fears,
Still losing when I saw myself to win!
What wretched errors hath my heart committed,
Whilst it hath thought itself so blessed never!
How have mine eyes out of their spheres been fitted,
In the distraction of this madding fever!
O benefit of ill! now I find true
That better is by evil still made better;
And ruin'd love, when it is built anew,
Grows fairer than at first, more strong, far greater.
    So I return rebuk'd to my content,
    And gain by ill thrice more than I have spent.

Edward bought a fine house in town befitting to the dignity of the Earl and Countess of Oxford. It was in the parish of St. Martin's in the Fields, hard by Cecil House where they had grown up together, and where Anne's parents were still living. Here they entertained the struggling poets, playwrights and actors of London, whose company Edward enjoyed at this time more than that of the courtiers at Whitehall. And here Anne lived a happy life as his gracious hostess.

Edward seems to be content to be with Anne again. We find among the Hatfield manuscripts a Latin poem copied from the flyleaf of her Greek Testament, written by Edward shortly before the birth of their second child. As in the sonnets, he puns on the Vere name and family motto, *Vero nil Verius.* "Nothing is truer than Truth," or "Nothing is truer than Vere,"—which Anne might have thought a slight exaggeration. Excerpts from this poem, translated, are: "Words of truth are fitting to a Vere." "Thou, a Vere, art wife and mother of a Vere (their daughter, Elizabeth) and seeing that thou mayst with good hope look forward with love of the truth and may thy true motto be Ever." (E. VERE) "Lover of the Truth."

Unfortunately the heir so eagerly anticipated, lived only two days. Two more children were born to them, but it must have been a disappointment that both were girls.

Shortly after Edward's return to Court in 1580, he had been involved in plots of the Catholic faction through his cousin, Lord Henry Howard, and Charles Arundel. He had even turned Catholic under their influence. However, he finally realized that involvement with them meant not only allegiance to Spain, but also a conspiracy against Queen Elizabeth. When faced with a choice of loyalties between family ties and the Queen, Edward invariably chose his Queen. So now he went to her and confessed all he knew about the plot. Acting on information he had given her, the Queen imprisoned Lord Howard and Arundel and even Edward himself for a brief period. But later he was appointed to sit as Judge at the court which condemned the conspirators to death. It is not pleasant to contemplate that Edward de Vere could so betray his blood cousin. Yet this was the sixteenth century, not the twentieth, and Lord Howard was the Queen's cousin, too. Through Edward's disclosures, Walsingham, head of the secret service, was enabled to take strong measures against other Catholic conspirators, which he had long wished to do to save the throne, but evidence was lacking. Edward's proof of loyalty seems to have impressed the Court as well as the Queen, and never again is it in question.

Indeed, in 1586 we find Edward sitting as one of the judges at the trial of Mary Queen of Scots.

Because of his vindication Oxford's financial situation, which had been precarious all through his early life, was now eased by his appointment in 1586 to an important government post by Walsingham with the Queen's approval and probably at her instigation. The post had to do with highly classified information in regard to affairs of state, and the salary was retroactive to some time before. It was said by contemporaries that the remuneration amounted to one per cent of the entire budget of the Kingdom, from which we may gauge the importance of the position. The grant lasted for the rest of his life, being renewed in the reign of James I. The nature of the work was never made public, nor was Oxford required to give an accounting of how the money was spent. This was the time that Shakespeare's history plays began to appear, which were known to have stirred up patriotic enthusiasm for the War with Spain. Is it too farfetched to believe that these plays were part of the work for which the Earl of Oxford was paid so munificently?

At least we can be glad that Anne was able to enjoy some of the comforts and luxuries she so richly deserved in these few years of married life with her adored lord. However, there is in the Hatfield manuscripts a letter from her father to Edward chiding him for overspending his income. Edward never did understand money; it came easily and slipped through his fingers. Still, though he spent lavishly, he gave away much of his substance, being ever softhearted toward his impecunious literary friends.

Lord Burghley writes of "my son-in-law's lewd companions." It is important to us to find out who these "lewd companions" were because it is highly possible that some or all of them at one time or another had a part in writing the famous plays.

In London in the latter quarter of the sixteenth century there were two rival literary groups: the Romanticists, whose leader was Sir Philip Sidney and which included Sir Edmund Spenser and Gabriel Harvey; and the Euphuists, who gathered about Edward, Earl of Oxford. It is this latter group which claims our interest, and it is quite true, as Lord Burghley intimated, that some of them lived far from exemplary private lives and that more than one knew the inside of London's prisons. But they were witty and creative, and researchers today profess to trace the hand of one or another of them in the plays we know as Shakespeare's.

The group included Christopher Marlowe, author of *Doctor Faustus, Edward II,* and other plays of marked success on the contemporary London stage; George Peele, dramatist, who wrote plays for the Children of the Chapel Royal, and who may have had a share in composing the first and second parts of *King Henry VI;* George Chapman,[1] poet, playwright, and translator of Homer, who

---

1. Oxford satirized Chapman's poetry in Sonnet 130, but it seems to have been all in good fun.

later saw service in the Low Countries under Edward's cousin, Sir Francis Vere; Thomas Nashe,[2] poet, dramatist and pamphleteer, called by a contemporary the "humerous critic of national manners," and who was also noted for his "sharp and satiric spirit;" Thomas Churchyard, the oldest of the group, who "wrote Songes and Sonnettes," and was sent by Edward to serve under the Prince of Orange, but was later disowned by his patron for some obscure reason. There is a possibility that Mary Sidney, Countess of Pembroke, came sometimes from Barnard Castle down the river to join in the scintillating conversation of these celebrated men. She was a poetess herself, a sister of Sir Philip Sidney, the leader of the rival school, who had written the *Arcadia* especially for her, and her presence in the Oxford circle points to the high place in English letters which Edward held among his contemporaries. Certain it is that, in the late years of the century, her two sons, the Earl of Pembroke and the Earl of Montgomery,[3] were among the visitors to the house near St. Martin's, since both young men were courting the younger de Vere daughters.

Two other famous authors of the day were undoubtedly members of the Oxford group, since both of them were private secretaries to Edward: John Lyly and Anthony Munday. Lyly, the lyric poet, author of *Euphues, or The Anatomy of Wit,* which gave the group its name,

2. In his Epistle Dedicatorie addressed to Oxford in 1593, Nashe wrote: "Yes, you have been such an infinite Maecenas to learned men . . . (who) have tasted the cool streams of your liberalitie . . . I would speak in commendation of your hospitalitie . . ."

3. The Earl of Pembroke and the Earl of Montgomery were the two most famous literary patrons of the succeeding age, "the incomparable pair of brethren" whom we shall meet again in the last chapter.

was called "the fiddle stick of Oxford." He also wrote eight plays for the Children of the Chapel Royal and the Children of St. Paul's, which were acted before the Queen, and will be referred to in our next chapter. Two of Liyly's plays were subsequently performed by the men actors at the Blackfriars Theatre. Munday, dramatist, traveller, journalist and possibly spy, was also an actor in the Earl of Oxford's Company of Players between 1579 and 1581. He collaborated with Drayton and other playwrights on *The First Part of the History and of the Life of Sir John Oldcastle,* which was, of course, the play from which *Henry IV* was taken. It was acted in 1599, printed in 1600 with the name, *William Shakespeare,* on the title page, but this was promptly withdrawn. In some ways Munday is the most appealing of the Euphuists. This is part of the letter he wrote to the Earl of Oxford when he left his employ to do service on the Continent in the War with Spain:

> My noble Master, farewell. May your desires, which are dear to us all, prevail. Earnestly do I pray for your welfare and success in the struggle. To the Guardianship of Christ I commit you and yours, till the day when, as Conquerors, we may peacefully resume our delightful literary discussions.

Of all that group centered about Edward, perhaps the most congenial to him was William Stanley, his future son-in-law, later the Earl of Derby. Like Edward, he was interested in the drama, and like Edward, he maintained a company of actors. We know from contemporary records that Edward and William Stanley were visiting each other in 1595, 1596 and 1598. And it might be noted here that Stanley's brother, Ferdinando, Lord Strange, was patron of the company of actors to which Shakespeare, the Stratford man, belonged.

There was not only good talk at the home of the Earl and Countess, but undoubtedly good music as well. "Musicyons" playing the lute, the virginals, the recorder, the viol, in concert or separately, used to perform for the aristocracy, and we have evidence that Edward, loving music as he did, enjoyed these intimate concerts. The plays are full of allusions to music. Here is the first line of *Twelfth Night:*

> If music be the food of love, play on.

I quote two more:

> The man that hath no music in himself,
> Nor is not moved with concord of sweet sounds,
> Is fit for treasons, strategems, and spoils.
> > *Merchant of Venice,* Act V, sc. 1.

> How sour sweet music is
> When time is broke, and no proportion kept!
> So is it in the music of men's lives.
> > *King Richard II,* Act V, sc. 5.

There was another form of music in which all the family and their assembled guests could join: madrigal singing. It is a pretty picture we have of the aristocratic Elizabethan family having supper usually about five-thirty in the afternoon. Winter evenings the Great Hall would be lighted by homemade candles on wooden or iron coronas suspended from the ceiling, casting flickering shadows on the wall tapestries. The floor of wood or stone was strewn with rushes. After supper the mistress of the house "was wont to serve out the part-books and call upon her guests to join with the family in singing madrigals." [4] Such was the setting which made "all England a nest of singing birds!"

John Farmer in 1599 published his *First Set of English Madrigals to Four Voices,* which he dedicated to the Earl of Oxford with these words among others:

> As a recreation your Lordship have overgrown most of them that make it (music) a profession.

The book contained seventeen numbers, including *Fair Phyllis I saw sitting all alone,* which is said to be a perfect little madrigal, and is characterized by delightful touches of realism. It has been suggested that Edward himself might have written some of the words set to Farmer's music, including, perhaps, the words to *Fair Phyllis.* We know that he composed madrigals, though unfortunately none have come down to us under his name.

But these halcyon days for the young countess were not to last. On June 5, 1588, Anne Cecil de Vere, Countess of Oxford, died at the age of thirty-three. She had led a harried life, but it is pleasant to record that in the last few years she had known true happiness with her lord. She was buried in Westminster Abbey, where her mother, Lady Burghley, was laid by her side a few months later. Lord Burghley, not the famous Earl of Oxford, composed the Latin inscription to commemorate his loss of these two "who were dear to him beyond the whole race of Womankind." Burghley himself is represented in the

---

4. *The English Madrigal,* Edmund H. Fellowes.

upper story of the tomb, kneeling in his robes of state as
Lord Treasurer, while Anne's three daughters, Elizabeth,
Bridget, and Susannah, kneel at their mother's head.
Anne lies on her tomb, a serene young woman with
auburn hair showing beneath her cap, dressed in a starched
ruff and bright red gown.

Of her distinguished husband no mention is made
at all.

Chapter IX

THE PLAYERS

"Alas! 'tis true I have gone here and there,
And made myself a motley to the view."
Sonnet 110.

Although it is our firm belief that the Earl of Oxford is the author of the famous plays we know as Shakespeare's, proof is impossible at this distance of four hundred years. Contemporary clues are tantalizing; they tell so much but leave so much untold. This story, however, is not intended to be a lawyer's brief but only a straight biography of the brilliant and fascinating Seventeenth Earl.

Interest in drama ran in the de Vere family. Indeed, the first record of an actors' troupe sponsored by an Earl of Oxford was in 1492, a date easy for Americans to remember.

The players mentioned in an earlier chapter sponsored

by the Sixteenth Earl [1] caused a scandal in 1547 by performing while a dirge was being played for King Henry VII at St. Saviour's.

Edward seems to have disbanded this company soon after his father's death, being at the time, we suppose, more concerned with his own education.

There is evidence that Oxford was associated with productions at Cambridge when he was a student. Also, he probably performed before the nobility at the Earl of Pembroke's Wilton House.

However, the first actual record we have of Edward taking part in a play himself is in 1579, when he was twenty-nine years old. We find that he played in a "Shrovetide device" at Court that year.

He must have maintained a troupe of players previous to 1580, because in that year we learn that the Earl of Warwick's men were transferred to Oxford's company, thereby laying themselves open to the charge of "fickleness."

This is the company that got into a fracas at the Inns of Court on April 12th, 1580. The Lord Mayor of London wrote to the Lord Chancellor about the disorder which he understood was already before the Privy Council. And on April 13th the Council committed three servants of Oxford to the Marshalsea Prison because of their part in the fray. They were Robert Leveson, Laurence Dutton (who seems prone to getting into trouble of this kind) and Thomas Chesson, but Chesson was released on bail. Because of this disturbance it was decided to get the players out of London as soon as possible and arrange for them to perform in the provinces.

---

1. For information in regard to the Earl of Oxford's players I am deeply indebted to E. K. Chambers' definitive book on *The Elizabethan Stage*, Vol. II, beginning at page 76.

We can trace the effort of Edward, sponsor of the troupe, in a letter of June 21st, 1580, from the Vice Chancellor of Cambridge University to Burghley, then Chancellor, acknowledging a letter from Burghley allowing Lord Oxford's men "to show their cunning in several plays already practised by them before the Queen's Majesty." We hear of them later that year in Norwich, and in Bristol in 1581; the troupe mentioned as playing in these two cities consisted of nine boys and one man. Probably the boys of the Earl's domestic Chapel travelled sometimes with the men players, while at other times they went about separately.

In 1584 we find a record of their first appearance at Court in a notation that the Earl of Oxford's "servauntes" performed January first, doubtless in connection with the Christmas revels, and they played there again the following March third. Their fee in both instances was paid to John Lyly, Edward's secretary, to be distributed by him afterward. The same troupe seems to have been in the provinces between 1583 and 1585, and is then described as "players" and "men."

But on December 27th, 1584, *Agamemnon and Ulysses* was played at Court by Oxford's "boys," and the performance was a part of the Christmas revels.

That same year we learn of a combination of Paul's Boys and the Children of the Chapel Royal playing at the Blackfriars Theatre under the direction of John Lyly, and this was the time that they performed Lyly's own plays. But after December, 1584, the Blackfriars reverted to Sir William More, and Lord Oxford seems to have had no more boys under his sponsorship.

He still maintained a company of men, his "servauntes," who performed at Court on January 1st, 1585, under the direction of John Symons, in feats of "activity and vaulting," those tumbling acts which the Elizabethans loved to watch. These tumblers had apparently been Lord Strange's men in 1583, and by 1586 they had left their patron, Oxford, and "returned" to the sponsorship of a still earlier patron, William Stanley.

That is the last record of Oxford's "plaiers" at Court. But Chambers finds them performing in Norwich again in 1585-6, in Ipswich in 1586-7, in London on January twenty-fifth, 1587, in York in June of 1587, and in Maidstone in 1589-90.

We have a letter from the privy Council to the Lord Mayor of London dated March 31st, 1602, to the effect that the Queen "has tolerated" a new company formed by the combination of Oxford's men and the Earl of Worcester's players and that they are at the Boar's Head, indicating that they have been there for some time previously.

Besides acting himself occasionally, Edward de Vere must have been a busy man these days, trying to keep an eye on the mischievous little boys and mettlesome young men of his Players' Companies, though he probably did not actually direct or manage the troupes himself. Still, he had decided ideas of how his actors should say their lines.

"Speak the speech, I pray you, as I pronounce it to you, trippingly on the tongue . . . Suit the action to the word, the word to the action, with this special observance, that you o'erstep not the modesty of nature," Hamlet tells the players, who doubtless declaimed and ranted as actors used to do in the medieval Miracle Plays. Edward would have none of that. His lines were to be recited by real people, and while he loved words, they were important to him only as they illuminated character or ideas.

We believe that he was also writing plays, both for his own companies to perform, and for other troupes.

74

Chapter X

POET AND PLAYWRIGHT

"So he that takes the pain to pen the book,
Reaps not the gifts of goodly golden muse;
But those gain that, who on the work shall look
And from the sour the sweet by skill shall choose."
Labour and Its Reward, by the young Earl of Oxford.

We have already seen some of Edward de Vere's early poetry, of which a sample is given above. A few more of his poems will be found at the end of this book. We know that he never signed a poem after he was twenty-six. Even though the examples of verse given here are rather crude—the effort of a young man trying out his pen— it is clear that the early works contain flashes of genius comparable to the poetry of Shakespeare. Oxford's words fall easily into poetic rhythm, while his imagination takes to picturesque metaphor. Is it likely that a young man so gifted would never write another line of poetry the rest of his life?

About the time that Edward had ceased to sign his name to poetry, Gilbert Talbot tells us that he wrote a play which was performed at Court. Can we ever forgive Talbot for not telling us what play that was!

It is thus only in passing references by contemporaries that we glean any clue to Oxford's literary output. In this brief biography we shall consider the plays and poetry together, since we are focussing mainly on the events of his life.

In 1586 William Webbe published his *Discourse on English Poetrie* in which the following sentence occurs:

> I may not omit the deserved commendations of many honourable and noble Lords and Gentlemen in her Majesty's Court, which in the rare devices of poetry have been and yet are most skilful; among whom the Right Honourable the Earl of Oxford may challenge to himself the title of the most excellent among the rest.

Lord Lumley mentions him in 1589 in his *Art of English Poetrie:*

> A crew of Courtly makers (poets), Noblemen, and Gentlemen, who have written excellently well, as it would appear if their doings could be found out and made public with the rest, of which number is first that noble Gentleman, the Earl of Oxford.

Note the phrase: "as it would appear if their doings could be found out and made public." The verb "could" indicates that there is some reason why Edward's poetry *could* not be made public.

That same year Sir Edmund Spenser published his *Tears of the Muses,* in which Oxford has been identified as the *Gentle Spirit.*

By 1598 a number of Shakespeare's plays had appeared. Yet Francis Meres wrote that

> The best for Comedy among us be Edward Earl of Oxford.

The question arises, then, why did not Oxford acknowledge authorship of the plays since so many of his contemporaries knew that he had written them?

The answer is not simple. First, let us admit that he must have signed his name to some plays, probably comedies, and that it is greatly to be regretted that these works have not been preserved for us. In a later chapter we shall consider some of the reasons why they were not.

Then it is probable that the plays Oxford did acknowledge were pleasant but innocuous works performed at Court, or at least, before an aristocratic audience. To the Elizabethans, this was acceptable and quite another thing from writing diverse plays for the general public to view. This latter was supposed to be quite beneath the dignity of a well-born nobleman.

But doubtless the main reason Oxford did not sign the greater number of his plays is that he *dared* not. To us the dramas of Shakespeare are delightful works of great literature. But to an Elizabethan many of them were thinly disguised and caustic comments on the times. Indeed, in most of Shakespeare's plays there were topical allusions apparent to any urbane playgoer, some instances even recognizable to the "groundlings."

Let us consider a few examples. *Love's Labours Lost,* one of the early plays, is a satire on Court life in which a number of allusions have been found to contemporary courtiers, and even to the Queen. So is *Twelfth Night*. Indeed, many of the scenes in Shakespeare depicting Court life must have been reflections of customs and people the author knew and frequently ridiculed. Remember that Hamlet refers to "the abstracts and brief chronicles of the time."

Or let us take *The Merchant of Venice*. An earlier play called variously *The History of Portia and Demorantes*, or *The Jew*, was known in London as far back as 1579. These early plays were given at small theatres like The Bull, or maybe in the courtyard of an Inn, before being presented at Court. Oxford was familiar with the sources of this play, and to them he added contemporary history, i.e., two episodes: the proposed marriage between the Duc d'Alençon and the Queen, and the third Frobisher Expedition. In the casket scene the author suggests to us the various suitors for the Queen's hand. The caskets themselves suggest the possession of the three crowns of iron, silver and gold, signifying the three countries of England, France and Ireland. Portia's words reflect a direct reference to the will of Henry VIII, which stipulated that the Queen should not marry without the consent of the Privy Council. Here is Portia's version:

> But this reasoning is not in the fashion to choose me a husband—O me, the word choose! I may neither choose whom I would, nor refuse whom I dislike; so is the will of a living daughter curbed by the will of a dead father.

The third Frobisher Expedition brought back metal purported to be gold, but which later was found to be worthless. Oxford had invested in this expedition, as we learned in an earlier chapter, having entered into a bond of which £2000 represented shares taken from one Lock, the accountant of the company, who, when the explorer returned, knew very well that the ore was worthless. For this offense he was sent to the Fleet Prison.

Now let us look at the characters: Portia, of course, represents the Queen; Antonio, the Earl of Oxford; Bassanio, d'Alencon; Lock, Shylock—the "shy" being in the sense of shady or disreputable. It is also worth noting that Antonio and Oxford entered into a bond for similar amounts, Antonio for 3,000 ducats, and Oxford for 3,000 pounds. Again, Shylock says:

> But ships are as boards, sailors but men; there be land-rats and water-rats; water-thieves and land-thieves; I mean pirates; and then there is the peril o' waters, winds and rocks. The man, notwithstanding, is sufficient: three thousand ducats: I think I may take his bond.

Edward had been attacked by pirates in 1576 and had also discharged one of his servants for fraud during his absence on the Continent. Hence, he had experienced both water-thieves and land-thieves. This is only one instance in which the author uses contemporary history in a play. Many more will occur to the reader.

Let us now consider some of the individual characters in Shakespeare's plays. We have mentioned before that Polonius would be recognized at once by a sophisticated audience as Lord Burghley—hardly a flattering portrayal of the illustrious Lord Treasurer of the Kingdom.

In 1580 a writer named Peck in his *Desiderata Curiosa* mentions,

a pleasant conceit of Vere, disappointed at the rising
of a mean gentleman in the English court circa 1580,

which could allude to the character of Malvolio in
Twelfth Night as a recognizable ridicule of Sir Christopher Hatton, who was noted for his fancy ways and
affected manner.

Even the envoys of the King of Spain seem to have
recognized a caricature of their royal master in a play
not named in the protest. There is today a letter from
Philip II in which he says that he is very much annoyed
by the accounts of "masques and comedies which the
Queen of England orders to be played at (his) expense."

It can be appreciated that such references as we have
cited would have been extremely dangerous for Oxford
had he claimed paternity to the famous plays. It were best
for him to live anonymously at Court bearing only his
proud title and its perquisites.

Chapter XI

EDWARD DE VERE II

"A son that well deserves
The honour and regard of such a father."
Two Gentlemen of Verona.

To Edward, the lonely, intense and imaginative intro-
vert, his relations with those close about him were as an
anchor in the gathering storms of life. We have already
touched upon his devotion to his father, his fluctuating
respect for his sovereign, and his congenial friendships
with the literary men of London. Deeper still were his
comforting affection for Anne Cecil during their short
years together, and his tortured infatuation with Anne
Vavasor which lasted through most of his life.

One other attachment was to be a strong influence
upon his character and a joy to his later years: his love
for Anne Vavasor's son, Edward. Having no legitimate
heir to his proud name and title, he turned to the bril-

liant and beguiling little boy with his mother, as she flitted from lover to husband and on to the next man. Oxford provided his financial support and was undoubtedly tempted to adopt him as his legal heir. But two good reasons frustrated that plan: first, the social stigma which would inevitably attach itself to Anne Cecil's family, and which would also be inimical to his own social and government positions. The other reason, even more compelling, was that the mother refused to part with the boy, since he was her chief source of income. Oxford at this time was selling off his estates in order to lavish luxuries upon his son.

Loving the boy so dearly and still under the bewitching spell of his scheming mother, Edward, not surprisingly after his wife died, went back to Anne Vavasor, now married to a sea captain named Finch, who conveniently left home for long voyages. Sonnet 152 tells of his ambivalent feelings toward her, and of a new torture, guilt:

> In loving thee thou know'st I am forsworn,
> But thou art twice forsworn, to me love swearing;
> In act thy bed-vow broke, and new faith torn,
> In vowing new hate after new love bearing.
> But why of two oaths' breach do I accuse thee,
> When I break twenty? I am perjur'd most;
> For all my vows are oaths but to misuse thee,
> And all my honest faith in thee is lost:
> For I have sworn deep oaths of thy deep kindness,
> Oaths of thy love, thy truth, thy constancy;
> And, to enlighten thee, gave eyes to blindness,
> Or made them swear against the thing they see;
> > For I have sworn thee fair; more perjur'd I,
> > To swear against the truth so foul a lie!

Is it not amazing how often Edward writes of *truth?* It seems to be ever in his mind.

For Oxford the years following Anne Cecil's death were beset with anxiety over his son and filled with acrimonious financial arguments with Lord Burghley, who was trying valiantly to save what he could of the de Vere estates. As Earl of Oxford, Edward had inherited not only Castle Hedingham, but eighty-five other estates, including two on the Avon, but they were slipping away from him fast these days. (The estates on the Avon could account for Ben Johnson's reference to "Sweet Swan of Avon!") It is assumed that these were the estates that had to be sold to pay Edward's debts. The last to go would have been Castle Hedingham, the ancestral home of the Earls of Oxford, where Edward had been brought up, and which he associated with his beloved father. But finally, that, too, had to be sold, and there is a record that the Earl of Oxford made over Castle Hedingham to his three daughters and their grandfather, Lord Burghley. And we note in *King Lear* that the king gives over his kingdom to his three daughters and that it went hard with him to do so.

Now once again Anne Vavasor has gone too far. In 1589 she gave birth to another son in Woodstock in the home of the father, old Sir Henry Lee,[1] her lover.

Edward reacted violently and irrationally to the idea of his own beloved eight-year-old son staying in Wood-

---

1. Recently the story of Anne Vavasor's living with Sir Henry Lee has come to light due to excellent detective work in the research of our American Shakespeare scholar, Charles Wisner Barrell, who found the record of a lawsuit brought against Anne by Sir Henry's nephew to recover certain treasures of his deceased uncle which Anne claimed had been given to her by the Earl of Oxford.

stock with his mother while she was living in open adultery with a man twice her age. In Sonnet 67 he tells how he resents this situation, mentioning the boy's rosy cheeks, which we know from his portraits. (Incidentally, both Anne Vavasor and Edward had high color.) Sonnet 67:

> Ah! wherefore with infection should he live,
> And with his presence grace impiety,
> That sin by him advantage should achieve
> And lace itself with his society?
> Why should false painting imitate his cheek,
> And steal dead seeing of his living hue?
> Why should poor beauty indirectly seek
> Roses of shadow, since his rose is true?
> Why should he live, now Nature bankrupt is,
> Beggar'd of blood, to blush through lively veins?
> For she hath no exchequer now but his,
> And, proud of many, lives upon his gains.
>> O, him she stores, to show what wealth she had
>> In days long since, before these last so bad.

Perhaps Edward recalled his own shame and anger when, as a young courtier, the Queen had taunted him for being a bastard. Reluctantly, he left the boy with his mother in the country where his parentage would not be questioned by prying inquisitors. But listen to Sonnet 36:

> Let me confess that we two must be twain,
> Although our undivided loves are one:
> So shall these blots that do with me remain,
> Without thy help, by me be borne alone.
> In our two loves there is but one respect,
> Though in our lives a separable spite,

Which, though it alter not love's sole effect,
Yet doth it steal sweet hours from love's delight.
I may not evermore acknowledge thee,
Lest my bewailed guilt should do thee shame,
Nor thou with public kindness honour me,
Unless thou take that honour from thy name:
    But do not so; I love thee in such sort
    As thou being mine, mine is thy good report.[1]

It was not until the youth was fifteen and ready for the university that he was finally separated from his mother. Edward thought wisely that, instead of sending him to Cambridge, his own university, he would arrange through his cousin, Sir Francis [2] to have him enter the University of Leyden, where the academic training was much the same as he would have received in England, all studies, both in England and on the Continent, being conducted in Latin.

Sir Francis, Oxford's cousin and great friend, was Commander-in-Chief of the English forces in the Netherlands, still fighting against the Spanish. It was said of him

---

1. For the suggestion of the relation of the sonnets to Edward's liaison with Anne Vavasor I am indebted to Professor Louis P. Benezet: *The Six Loves of "Shake-speare."* Professor Benezet believes that more than forty of "Shake-speare's" sonnets are addressed by the Earl of Oxford to his distinguished and dearly loved son.

2. Sir Francis comes vividly to life for us, ironically, when we see his tomb in the North Transept of Westminster Abbey. He is buried in one tomb with his brother, Horatio, Baron Vere of Tilbury. The recumbent effigy of Sir Franiis lies on a slab of black marble, with his cloak wrapped around him like a Roman toga. Four kneeling knights support another black marble slab above him, on which rest pieces of his armor. These four statues seem so utterly alive that one is tempted to listen to hear them speak.

that he "brought more glory to the name of Vere than he took of blood from the family of Oxford." And again he was described as "a gentleman of singular character, both for arms and letters."

Edward has written a series of beautiful sonnets to his young son. Here is Number 26:

> Lord of my love, to whom in vassalage
> Thy merit hath my duty strongly knit,
> To thee I send this written ambassage
> To witness duty, not to show my wit:
> Duty so great, which wit so poor as mine
> May make seem bare, in wanting words to show it,
> But that I hope some good conceit of thine
> In thy soul's thought, all naked, will bestow it;
> Till whatsoever star that guides my moving
> Points on me graciously with fair aspect,
> And puts apparel on my tatter'd loving,
> To show me worthy of thy sweet respect:
> > Then may I dare to boast how I do love thee;
> > Till then, not show my head where thou mayst
> > prove me.

And Sonnet 44, written to Edward at school on the Continent:

> If the dull substance of my flesh were thought,
> Injurious distance should not stop my way;
> For then despite of space, I would be brought,
> From limits far remote, where thou dost stay.
> No matter then although my foot did stand
> Upon the furthest earth remov'd from thee;
> For nimble thought can jump both sea and land,
> As soon as think the place where he would be.
> But ah! thought kills me that I am not thought,

William Cecil, First Baron Burghley.

By courtesy of the National Portrait Gallery.

Edward de Vere, Earl of Oxford, aged twenty-four.

The Welbeck Portrait, by an unknown Flemish artist, in the collection of the Duke of Portland, on loan to the National Portrait Gallery.

By courtesy of the Duke of Portland.

Queen Elizabeth, 1575.

Drawing by Federigo Zuccaro.

By courtesy of The British Museum.

Lord Burghley Presiding at the Court of Wards and Liveries, 1585.

By courtesy of the Trustees of the Goodwood Collection.

Lines of correction of the play, *Sir Thomas More*, considered by the scholars to be in the handwriting of the famous playwright.

By courtesy of The British Museum.

To leap large lengths of miles when thou are gone;
But that, so much of earth and water wrought,
I must attend time's leisure with my moan;
 Receiving nought by elements so slow
 But heavy tears, badges of either's woe.

Another, Sonnet 45, tells of his being "oppress'd with melancholy" till the messengers from young Edward return with news of him:

The other two, slight air and purging fire,
Are both with thee, wherever I abide;
The first my thought, the other my desire,
These present-absent with swift motion slide.
For when these quicker elements are gone
In tender embassy of love to thee,
My life, being made of four, with two alone
Sinks down to death, oppress'd with melancholy;
Until life's composition be recur'd
By those sweet messengers return'd from thee,
Who even but now come back again, assur'd
Of thy fair health, recounting it to me:
 This told, I joy; but then no longer glad,
 I send them back again, and straight grow sad.

What heartbreak for the father not to be able to be with his son!

After two years at the university the lad, now grown to be a handsome, stalwart young man, left his studies to join the English army under the command of his guardian, Sir Francis, who soon appointed him captain of a company of pikemen.

Then came news to his father that he had been decorated for gallantry in action! A true de Vere! And the proud father wrote to him this sonnet, Number 37:

As a decrepit father takes delight
To see his active child do deeds of youth,
So, I, made lame by fortune's dearest spite,
Take all my comfort of thy worth and truth:
For whether beauty, birth, or wealth, or wit,
Or any of these all, or all, or more,
Entitled in thy parts do crowned sit,
I make my love engrafted to this store:
So then I am not lame, poor, nor despis'd,
Whilst that this shadow doth such substance give
That I in thy abundance am suffic'd
And by a part of all thy glory live.
    Look what is best, that best I wish in thee;
    That wish I have: then ten times happy me!

Subsequently young Edward de Vere was knighted by King James, and still later became a respected Member of Parliament. A gifted writer of poems and plays, his heroes, it is worth noting, were frequently illegitimate sons.

Sir Edward de Vere was killed in action in the Battle of Bois-le-Duc before he was fifty years old.

Chapter XII

SOUTHAMPTON

That beauty still may live in thine or thee.
Make thee another self, for love of me,
                                        Sonnet 10.

We know from the records that in the Battle of the
Spanish Armada in November, 1588, which was five
months after Anne Cecil died, Edward fitted out a war-
ship at his own expense and became its captain, naming
his ship *The Edward Bonaventure* in contrast to Drake's
ship, *The Elizabeth Bonaventure*. His reward from his
grateful sovereign was the honor of riding by her side
in the triumphal procession to St. Paul's to celebrate the
victory with Thanksgiving. In the Cathedral, as Lord
Great Chamberlain and Senior Earl, he and the Earl
of Shrewsbury, the Earl Marshal, bore the golden canopy
over the Queen as she walked in solemn dignity to her
chair of honor in the choir. Edward refers to this incident

almost contemptuously in a sonnet later, for the honors of Court life had ceased to appeal to him compared to the love and security of a happy home.

The year after the Armada battle, in 1589, the great Sturmius, leader of the German Protestants, addressed an urgent plea to Queen Elizabeth to send over "the Earl of Oxford, or the Earl of Leicester, or Sir Philip Sidney" to the Low Countries, in an effort to repel the Spanish invader, and to stem the rising tide of Catholicism on the Continent. This request came to Elizabeth before Sir Francis Vere took over the English forces there, as described in the previous chapter.

The Queen dispatched Oxford to serve as Commander of Cavalry under Sir John Norris,[1] Commander in Chief. Edward was most anxious to go; he yearned for military glory. But the Earl of Leicester, in a rage of jealousy at being left behind, prevailed upon the Queen to send a civilian to take the orders to Norris and Oxford, thereby undercutting their authority and sowing dangerous dissention in the ranks of the troops. After only three months Edward was recalled, to his bitter disappointment. Sir Philip Sidney was sent over first, then Leicester was finally given the post of Commander in Chief of the English Forces, which he had so cleverly wangled. It was an unfortunate appointment for him, for he was in

---

1. The tomb of Sir John Norris is in Westminster Abbey not far from the tomb of his sovereign, Queen Elizabeth. We mention the tombs of Sir John, and of Sir Francis Vere, because of the life-like figures on them, giving us, even four hundred years later, a sense of having seen these famous soldiers. A. L. Rowse, in *The England of Elizabeth,* writes: "The two Norris brothers, the most admired soldiers of the time, Black John and his brother, Tom in whose arms John dies, are to be seen in Westminster Abbey: their figures the masterpieces of that most expressive sculptor, Isaac James."

no way equal to its demands. And Sir Philip, his illustrious nephew, met death after being wounded at the Battle of Zutphen.

Upon returning home, Edward found plenty of family problems to occupy his mind. His oldest daughter, Elizabeth, was approaching marriageable age, and in 1590 there began negotiations to marry her to Henry Wriothesley, Third Earl of Southampton. Henry was the only child of a doting, widowed and ambitious countess, who was eager for this union of her son with the daughter of the Premier Earl of the Realm, not to mention that she was the granddaughter of the Lord Treasurer, Burghley. That scheming old gentleman was also favorable to the marriage, as many a letter from him to the young earl existing today at Hatfield can attest. And Edward, Earl of Oxford, with no legitimate heir, was perhaps most anxious of all for this match between his daughter and the personable young aristocrat. Moreover, Southampton was a rich and much-sought-after bachelor with long fair curls and deep blue eyes, "the world's fresh ornament."

He was the right age for Elizabeth de Vere, being just two years older than she, and the two families had known each other as neighbors on the Strand. Wriothesley, like Edward, had been a Royal Ward brought up by Lord Burghley, and he had succeeded to his title at an even younger age than Edward, when he was only eight years old. The elder nobleman and the younger would have had much in common, for Southampton, being enormously wealthy, had been a munificent patron of poets and authors, including Nashe, Markham, Barnebe Barnes and John Florio, the latter becoming a member of his household and teaching him Italian.

Southampton also took a considerable share in pro-

91

moting colonial enterprises and was an active member of the Council of the Virginia Company.

And, like Oxford, he loved drama. Rowland White wrote to Sir Robert Sidney that "my Lord Southampton and Lord Rutland come not to Court . . . They pass away the time in London merely in going to plays every day."

However, the character of this young nobleman stands out from the other courtiers of the Queen because of his strange and insidious charm which attracted to him both men and women. This attraction is hard to understand from studying his portraits, which show only a fastidious and effeminate young man, but it seems to have been the quality which shaped his career. Early in life he attached himself to Robert Devereux, Earl of Essex, another Royal Ward who had been brought up by Lord Burghley. Essex rose to the highest eminence to which a courtier could aspire: favorite of the Queen. Southampton was five years younger than Essex and doubtless their friendship began while they were living as wards at Cecil House.

Subsequently we find Southampton by the side of Essex at Cadiz and the Azores, and again in 1599 in the unfortunate Irish Expedition. In Ireland Essex created his young friend General of the Horse, but the Queen, very angry at hearing about the honors Essex was bestowing right and left, made him retract the title and recalled Southampton to London. And we find him at Essex House, that great mansion overlooking the Thames, where the two ambitious and disloyal young earls drafted the incriminating letters to King James of Scotland and later planned the March on London.

But all this was in the future, that year of 1590, when negotiations began regarding the marriage between Elizabeth de Vere and this irresponsible but exotic young man. During the four years that the negotiations were in progress, the Earl of Oxford's contribution was a series of sonnets.[2]

The first explains his position:

From fairest creatures we desire increase,
That thereby beauty's rose might never die,
But the the riper should by time decease,
His tender heir might bear his memory:
But thou, contracted to thine own bright eyes,
Feed'st thy light's flame with self-substantial fuel,
Making a famine where abundance lies,
Thyself thy foe, to thy sweet self too cruel.
Thou that art now the world's fresh ornament
And only herald to the gaudy spring,
Within thine own bud buriest thy content
And, tender churl, mak'st waste in niggarding.
    Pity the world, or else this glutton be,
    To eat the world's due, by the grave and thee.

Edward was forty in 1590. In the second sonnet he wrote to Southampton, twenty-two years younger:

When forty winters shall besiege thy brow,
And dig deep trenches in thy beauty's field,
Thy youth's proud livery, so gazed on now,
Will be a tatter'd weed, of small worth held:
Then being ask'd where all thy beauty lies,
Where all the treasure of thy lusty days,
To say, within thine own deep-sunken eyes,
Were an all-eating shame and thriftless praise.
How much more praise deserv'd thy beauty's use,

---

2. Again I am indebted to Professor Louis P. Benezet for much of the interpretation of the sonnets.

93

If thou couldst answer, 'This fair child of mine
Shall sum my count, and make my old excuse,'
Proving his beauty by succession thine!
This were to be new made when thou art old,
And see thy blood warm when thou feel'st it cold.

There were fifteen more of these sonnets that have
come down to us, and possibly many others now lost. One,
the third, is a gesture to the widowed countess, Southampton's mother:

Thou art thy mother's glass, and she in thee
Calls back the lovely April of her prime:
So thou through windows of thine age shalt see,
Despite of wrinkles, this thy golden time.
But if thou live, remember'd not to be,
Die single, and thine image dies with thee.

Other sonnets chide the young man for his "self-will"
and love of flattery. Southampton finally agreed to a
formal betrothal, but he balked at marriage, having by
this time discovered the charms of another Maid of Honor
to the Queen, Elizabeth Vernon, a cousin of the Earl of
Essex.

Just after the betrothal was announced, a poem appeared called *Venus and Adonis,* dedicated in most formal
language to *The Right Honourable Henry Wriothesley,
Earl of Southampton,* and signed by a name never before
seen in print: *William Shake-speare.*

It is, of course, quite possible that Oxford appropriated
the name as a nom de plume. It is more likely, however,
that, quite independently, he chose a name suggested by
the Bolebec crest. It will be remembered that Edward was
Viscount Bolebec as well as Earl of Oxford and that the

Bolebec crest was a lion brandishing a broken spear. When in 1578 Gabriel Harvey had so extravagantly praised Oxford's composition Harvey used the phrase *Vultas tela vibrat,* "Thy countenance shakes spears," which is thought to be a pun on the pen name *already* adopted by Oxford and doubtless recognized by those in the know.

The dedication to *Venus and Adonis* [3] is put in deferential language as was the custom of the age, but there is appended a Latin couplet from the *Amores* of Ovid, which, translated, reads: "Let the rabble enjoy cheap pleasures. For me let yellow haired Apollo serve cups filled from the spring of the Muses." In contrast to the dedication, this comes from a social equal—a cultured gentleman writing to another cultured gentleman, in this respect, similar to the sonnets written to the same earl.

Sonnet 82 refers to Oxford's dedication of the poem to Southampton:

> I grant thou wert not married to my Muse,
> And therefore mayst without attaint o'erlook
> The dedicated words which writers use,
> Of their fair subject, blessing every book.

Some months after *Venus and Adonis* appeared, a second poem, *The Rape of Lucrece,* came out. This also was dedicated to the Earl of Southampton, and over the same signature, *William Shake-speare.* Only this time there was no mention of *Right Honourable,* but only a salute of one nobleman to a brother nobleman:

---

3. This explanation is also taken from Professor Benezet's book on the sonnets mentioned before.

The love I dedicate to your Lordship is without end.

Six months after this dedication the love did come to an end, when the friendship between the Earl of Oxford and the young man he had chosen for his son-in-law, was abruptly broken off. Sonnet 144 gives the reason:

Two loves I have of comfort and despair,
Which like two spirits do suggest me still:
The better angel is a man right fair,
The worser spirit a woman, colour'd ill.
To win me soon to hell, my female evil
Tempteth my better angel from my side,
And would corrupt my saint to be a devil,
Wooing his purity with her foul pride.
And whether that my angel be turn'd fiend
Suspect I may, but not directly tell;
But being both from me, both to each friend,
I guess one angel in another's hell;
    Yet this shall I ne'er know, but live in doubt,
    Till my bad angel fire my good one out.

What does this mean? It means that Anne Vavasor [4] is "on the prowl again," and that she has set her cap for the rich young earl. She is twenty-eight now, while Southampton is just twenty. Anne has two sons, while Southampton has become rather involved with Elizabeth Vernon. But Anne still has the come-hither in her eye, and once more Edward de Vere is consumed with jealousy. Sonnet 41 tells of the climax:

Those pretty wrongs that liberty commits,
When I am sometimes absent from thy heart,
Thy beauty and thy years full well befits,

---

4. The reader will recall that Southampton had light hair and Anne Vavasor is always referred to as "dark."

For still temptation follows where thou art.
Gentle thou art, and therefore to be won,
Beauteous thou art, therefore to be assailed;
And when a woman woos, what woman's son
Will sourly leave her till she have prevailed?
Ay me! but yet thou mightst my seat forbear,
And chide thy beauty and thy straying youth
Who lead thee in their riot even there
Where thou art forc'd to break a twofold truth—
    Hers, by thy beauty tempting her to thee,
    Thine, by thy beauty being false to me.

Again note the harping on *truth*. But what can this sonnet mean? It is simply that Southampton had had the temerity to have an assignation with Anne Vavasor in Edward's own house while he was absent! Doubtless both Wriothesley and Anne Vavasor had frequently been guests of Edward at one or another of his estates. But the insolence of this offense cannot be ignored. It has been an inexcusable breach of friendship.

Southampton uses this sonnet as reason to break off the betrothal with Edward's daughter. And old Burghley, trustee of his granddaughter's estate, demands a forfeit from Henry Wriothesley for refusing to marry the girl! The facts we know lead into the assumptions which we cannot prove.

Southampton finally married Elizabeth Vernon, but not until a few months before the birth of her child. One more of the Queen's Ladies in Waiting had ceased to be a Maid of Honour! And both Southampton and Elizabeth Vernon, with their child, were sent to the Fleet Prison.

But Edward de Vere, so unfortunate in his relationships, wrote a final poem to the young man he had chosen for his son-in-law, and for whom there is no denying he had developed a rather more than father-in-law interest. Sonnet 87:

> Farewell! Thou art too dear for my possessing,
> And like enough thou know'st thy estimate:
> The charter of thy worth gives thee releasing;
> My bonds in thee are all determinate.
> For how do I hold thee but by thy granting?
> And for that riches where is my deserving?
> The cause of this fair gift in me is wanting,
> And so my patent back again is swerving.
> Thyself thou gav'st, thy own worth then not knowing,
> Or me, to whom thou gav'st it, else mistaking;
> So thy great gift, upon misprision growing,
> Comes home again, on better judgment making.
>   Thus have I had thee, as a dream doth flatter,
>   In sleep a king, but, waking no such matter.

The Lady Elizabeth de Vere was allowed to marry the suitor of her choice, her father's great friend, William Stanley, Earl of Derby. They will come into our story several times again. Their wedding was one of the great occasions of the London season of 1595. The marriage was performed on January twenty-sixth, probably in the Chapel of the Savoy Palace, since neither St. Martin's nor St. Clement Danes has the record. But we do have record that the wedding reception was held at Cecil House, home of the Lord Treasurer, grandfather of the bride. Moreover, we also know that the Queen came in all the way from Greenwich, where she was then holding Court, to be present for the festivities because the Church Wardens of St. Martin's record this entry:

> Item paid the XXXth of January for ringing
> At her Majesties comynge to ye Lord Treasurers
> to ye Earle of Darbies wedding And at her De-
> parture from thence ye sixth of ffebruary ijs.

So there were seven days of festivities in the cold and dreary month of January! And we know that on one of those days *A Midsummer Night's Dream* was performed in the presence of her Majesty.[5] It had been composed especially for this celebration.[6]

---

5. *Shakespeare Gleanings*, by E. K. Chambers.
6. The musk rose mentioned in *Midsummer Night's Dream* was brought to England by Gerard, Lord Burghley's famous gardener.

Chapter XIII

ELIZABETH TRENTHAM

"You are my all-the-world!"
Sonnet 112.

Following the death of Anne Cecil, Edward's melancholy mood returned, aggravated by Burghley's continual chiding on finance, the vain attempt to win Southampton for his daughter, and the ever-present anxiety on behalf of Edward, his son.

It is hardly surprising that he sought refuge with Anne Vavasor, though hating himself for his weakness in once again succumbing to her wiles. All this must have troubled his oldest daughter, Elizabeth de Vere, then in the midst of her own love affair with William Stanley. Also, there were the two younger sisters to bring up. Whether Elizabeth de Vere is responsible for introducing her friend, Elizabeth Trentham, to her father, we do not know. We do know, however, that Edward was soon seeking consolation with this lovely Maid in Waiting to the Queen, so different from the last one he had courted. She was the daughter of Sir Thomas Trentham, a wealthy Staffordshire landowner, famous for her beauty, and about the age of her suitor's eldest daughter. She seems to have fallen deeply in love with the forty-one-year-old statesman, playwright and poet who never did lose his skill to charm the ladies. Here are two sonnets Edward must have written to Elizabeth Trentham while he was courting her. Sonnet number 125:

> Were 't aught to me I bore the canopy,
> With my extern the outward honouring,
> Or laid great bases for eternity,
> Which prove more short than waste or ruining?
> Have I not seen dwellers on form and favour
> Lose all and more by paying too much rent,
> For compound sweet forgoing simple savour,
> Pitiful thrivers, in their gazing spent?
> No; let me be obsequious in thy heart,
> And take thou my oblation, poor but free,
> Which is not mix'd with seconds, knows no art,
> But mutual render, only me for thee.
> > Hence, thou suborn'd informer! a true soul
> > When most impeach'd stands least in thy control.

We recall that Oxford with the Earl of Shrewsbury had held the golden canopy over the Queen at the Service of Thanksgiving after the Armada victory. Doubtless he had done so on other important occasions, since it was one of his duties as Lord Great Chamberlain and Senior Earl. But Elizabeth Trentham would have known about the great service at St. Paul's only three years before, and she understood when he told her so eloquently that the coveted honor meant nothing to him compared

101

to the honor of loving her. He goes on to recount that he, himself, had "laid great bases for eternity" which had not lasted at all. He had seen courtiers risk all—"pay too much rent"—"and lose all and more." "Pitiful thrivers," he calls them. And never again will he be obsequious; had he ever been, we wonder? He offers his oblation to his goddess, Elizabeth, in complete surrender. And again he refers to "a true soul"—E. VERE. How much of himself he packs into those fourteen lines!

Here is another sonnet to Elizabeth, number 112:

Your love and pity doth the impression fill
Which vulgar scandal stamp'd upon my brow;
For what care I who calls me well or ill,
So you o'er-green my bad, my good allow?
You are my all-the-world, and I must strive
To know my shames and praises from your tongue;
None else to me, nor I to none alive,
That my steel'd sense or changes right or wrong.
In so profound abysm I throw all care
Of voices, that my adder's sense
To critic and to flatterer stopped are.
Mark how with my neglect I do dispense:
    You are so strongly in my purpose bred
    That all the world besides me methinks are dead.

The "vulgar scandal" must refer to the gossip about himself and Anne Vavasor, which doubtless became exaggerated each time it was repeated in Court circles. Elizabeth Trentham would have heard about it, yet she knew her man, and knew she could trust him to be faithful to her if she gave herself to him. Never again do we hear of Anne Vavasor coming into Edward's life. His surrender to Elizabeth is complete.

Yet the sensitive lover still feels guilt because of his past life, and he must confess to Elizabeth his laxities in Sonnet 110. He admits also that he has been an actor! This rumor had already scandalized old Burghley, as we know from his letters about it. My son-in-law an actor!—"a motley to the view"? Terrible! And here Edward is writing about it quite casually to the girl he is about to marry! Sonnet 110:

> Alas! 'tis true I have gone here and there,
> And made myself a motley to the view,
> Gor'd mine own thoughts, sold cheap what is most dear,
> Made old offences of affections new;
> Most true it is that I have look'd on truth
> Askance and strangely; but, by all above,
> These blenches gave my heart another youth,
> And worse essays prov'd thee my best of love.
> Now all is done, have what shall have no end:
> Mine appetite I never more will grind
> On newer proof, to try an older friend,
> A god in love, to whom I am confin'd.
> > Then give me welcome, next my heaven the best,
> > Even to thy pure and most most loving breast.

Perhaps Edward de Vere regrets most of all that he has "look'd on truth askance and strangely!" Yet the last two beautiful lines prove that he no longer regrets the past.

Note how different in tone are the sonnets to Elizabeth Trentham from those addressed to Anne Vavasor. In the earlier poems we feel Edward's hot blood and uncontrollable passion, while these beautiful later sonnets are the outpouring of a middle-aged lover happy in anticipation of a quiet life with his loved one.

Edward and Elizabeth Trentham were quietly married in 1591 and went to live in Stoke Newington, a suburb of London, more congenial to the retired life the bride and bridegroom wanted than the great mansion in St. Martin's parish. And Stoke Newington was near the theatres!

There followed twelve years of utter devotion to one another. Also, Elizabeth's inheritance greatly assisted Edward's financial situation.

In 1593 his Countess presented him with the legitimate son he had so longed for all his life. Henry de Vere grew up to be a comely youth, though he never wrapped himself around his father's heartstrings as Edward, his other son, had done. However, it seems that Sonnet 126 is written to this little boy, his heir:

O thou, my lovely boy, who in thy power
Dost hold Time's fickle glass, his sickle hour;
Who hast by waning grown, and therein show'st
Thy lovers withering as thy sweet self grow'st;
If Nature, sovereign mistress over wrack,
As thou goest onwards, still will pluck thee back,
She keeps thee to this purpose, that her skill
May time disgrace and wretched minutes kill.
Yet fear her, O thou minion of her pleasure!
She may detain, but not still keep her treasure:
    Her audit, though delay'd, answer'd must be,
    And her quietus is to render thee.

In 1596 the family moved again, this time to the estate of the Countess: King's Place, Hackney.[1]

Meanwhile the little girls were growing up, torn between their love and loyalty to their father and the pomp-

---

1. This house remained standing until the last war, but was so badly bombed in the blitz that it had to be torn down.

ous effort of their grandfather and later, their uncle Robert Cecil, to alienate them from him. Elizabeth Trentham de Vere would have her hands full with them, and she must have been relieved when each girl became betrothed. Susan, the younger, was married first, to the Earl of Montgomery, while Bridget, after a long betrothal to the Earl of Pembroke, Montgomery's brother, finally married Francis, Lord Norris, afterward the Earl of Berkshire.

However, it would be natural to assume that the Earl and Countess of Derby would be the closest to Edward and his Countess, the Earl being an old friend and nearer the age of Edward, while Elizabeth de Vere Stanley had been a special friend of Elizabeth Trentham de Vere, her present stepmother. Derby himself was the center of a literary circle and also wrote both plays and poetry. We can perhaps picture the two couples gathered about the lamplight before the big open fireplace reading aloud to each other in the long winter evenings, the two young women with their embroidery, the two authors revising, rewriting and polishing their plays.

Literary fame was now coming to Edward. In 1598 Francis Meres recorded in that somewhat confusing passage referred to in an earlier chapter, that Oxford was "the best for comedy," mentioning also William Shakespeare and twelve of his plays, as well as *Venus and Adonis*, *Lucrece*, and "his sugar'd sonnets among his private friends." This passage, which is one of the strongest arguments of the orthodox school in proving that the Stratford man and Oxford were two different people, is explained by the Ogburns [2] thus:

---

2. *Shake-speare, the Man Behind the Name*, by Dorothy and Charlton Ogburn, Jr., page 37.

The inclusion of Oxford along with Shakespeare, taken by some to indicate that he was a different person, is explicable on the grounds that he (Oxford) was too well known as a dramatist in his own right to be excluded—certainly without exciting suspicion.

Nashe had already said of Lord Oxford: "Mark him well. He hath one of the best wits in England." Lumley, also mentioned before, names him as one of England's two best writers of "Comedy and Enterludes."

Edward de Vere's biography would be incomplete without recording how he appeared to his contemporaries. We have already noted that George Chapman has given us a picture of him as a young nobleman travelling on the Continent in great style. Note the vivid details:

> . . . He had a face
> Like one of the honour'd Romans
> From whence his noblest family was deriv'd . . .
> Valiant, and learn'd and liberal as the sun.

No wonder Edward never had any money! All his life he had been too liberal in passing it out!

How did he appear to his own retainers? One of them, Andrew Trollop, in 1587, wrote to Lord Burghley:

> From the 10th to the 31st year of her majesty I was Deputy to Thomas Gent, esquire; then steward of the manors of the Right Honourable the Earl of Oxford, and during all the time being privy, not only of his public dealings, but also of his private doings and secret intents, found and knew him endued with special piety, perfect integrity, great desire to discharge all trust reposed in him, and no less desire to do good in the commonwealth.

106

A fine tribute from one of his own servants! Let us hope that it impressed his father-in-law!

And now let us see how Lord Burghley did regard his son-in-law, Edward de Vere, Earl of Oxford. Apparently Burghley considered him his own son during the period when he was guardian. Later, after his faithlessness to Anne Cecil, Burghley and Oxford exchanged many bitter words on paper and, presumably, orally. Edward's improvidence must have been exasperating to the older man. Moreover, their personalities were poles apart, Oxford so irresponsible, and Burghley so wise and caretaking. Yet before he died, Burghley gave this grudging tribute to the younger man:

> In matters of thrift inconsiderate, but resolute in dutifulness to the Queen and his country.

The biographer who tells the mere facts of the life of a famous man falls far short of explaining him to anyone else. Whole libraries have been written about Shakespeare, yet how little we really know about the playwright. What was it that moved him to compose the timeless dramas? What forces sustained him through stress and strain?

We have suggested that the love and good will of his friends and family were of prime importance to Edward de Vere. And as we read his works we know how deeply he believed in Truth. Indeed, many of the great plays are built around that theme. And so we are tempted to ask with Pilate, What is Truth? and seek with Francis Bacon to find the answer. But the answer is elusive.

Oxford, we know, owned the Geneva Bible. Frequently it is quoted in his poetry, in the sonnets and in the plays. There are allusions to Christian doctrines and Christian imagery. Yet in extremity the Shakespearean hero seems loath to rely on Christian belief. Rather is he sustained by the philosophy of the Stoics. Men must endure their going hence, even as their coming hither, counsels Edgar in *King Lear*. Is this the philosophy of the master playwright? If so, the virtues he extols are endurance and fortitude, rather than faith in the supernatural.

Oxford, we know, was well acquainted with John Florio, who was a member of the household of the Earl of Southampton and one of the Euphuists, belonging to the inner circle of the Oxford group. John Florio had translated Montaigne's Essays into English. Like our English playwright, the French man of letters was conservative and agnostic, given to appreciation of the pleasures of this world, and his inquisitive mind would accept no opinion untried. He enjoyed living to the full, yet he had no fear of dying, hoping above all else, he told his readers, that he would die "quietly and constantly."

This may cast a thin ray of light on the inner soul of the author of the greatest tragedies ever written in the English language.

Note: For material used in this chapter bearing directly on Oxford's relations with his second wife, Elizabeth Trentham, I am once again deeply indebted to the original research of Professor Louis P Benezet.

Chapter XIV

BURGHLEY

"And these few precepts in thy memory
See thou character. Give thy thoughts no tongue,
Nor any unproportioned thought his act."
                    Polonius to Laertes, in *Hamlet.*

Running through our story of Edward de Vere like a gray thread weaving through cloth of gold is the story of his former guardian and father-in-law, Baron Burghley, the Lord Treasurer of the Realm. We met him first at Castle Hedingham as the young Queen's Principal Secretary. We came to know him better as guardian to the youthful Royal Ward, Edward, when he came to live at Cecil House. It is only fair to record that he gave his ward an excellent education, guiding him to the type of learning which would be most useful to him in his future career. And we have evidence that he was sincerely fond of his young charge in those days. But from what we know of guardian and ward, it seems inevitable that their temperaments should clash sooner or later. Naturally our story, written from the viewpoint of Edward, gives a somewhat distorted picture. To see Lord Burghley more clearly, and to understand his influence on Edward and Edward's children, let us bring his career into focus.

In 1591 Lord Burghley tendered his resignation to the Queen. His reason was ill-health, gout and "stomach trouble," aggravated by grief in the death of his wife and daughter, Anne. He was at this time seventy-one; he felt he deserved a few years of retirement.

But the Queen, "who saw no decay in his abilities and who willingly granted all the indulgences possible to his infirmities," refused to accept his resignation. In a letter "written with great wit and spirit (she) diverted him absolutely from his serious purpose." How could she ever reign without her faithful "Spirit"? He alone of all the courtiers was granted the privilege of sitting down in her presence, while the others stood or knelt on one knee when addressing her.

"My Lord, we make much of you," she said, "not for your bad legs but for your good head."

The famous statesman who was "Sir Spirit" to the Queen was born at Bourn, Lincolnshire, in 1520. His father, Sir Richard Cecyll, of Burley, in Northamptonshire, had begun his career at Court as page to King Henry VIII. Hence, father and son had not only lived through the exciting events of all but one of the Tudor reigns, but had had a determining influence on most of them. If one may anticipate a little, and consider also Lord Burghley's son, Sir Robert Cecil, we may record one family giving three generations of service to four English monarchs, unparalleled in any other instance.

Sir Richard Cecyll, or Cecil, as the name came to be

spelled, had been Steward of the King's Manors and Constable of Warwick Castle, though his longest service to Henry VIII was as Master of the Robes. In this latter capacity he had attended his gorgeous Majesty at the Field of the Cloth of Gold in 1520, the year William, his famous son, was born. On the death of Richard Cecil he was buried with honors in St. Margaret's, Westminster.

As a young man ambitious for preferment, William Cecil had searched his antecedents for a peerage, but in vain. Instead of noble blood and great riches, his Herefordshire ancestors bequeathed to him a profound rather than a brilliant intellect, great wisdom and a tremendous capacity for application. It was written of Cecil that "in his infancy (he was) so pregnant in wit, and so desirous and apt to learn, as in expectation foretold his great future fortune."

At fifteen we find that he graduated from St. John's College, Cambridge. And while he was a student there, we note that he hired the bell ringer to waken him at four in the morning, so that he could study without interruption until chapel time. But unfortunately his erudition came at a high price; his poring over books and lack of exercise undermined his health, leading to the gout which plagued him the rest of his life.

Contemporaries of his at Cambridge included Sir Thomas Smith, whom we met as Edward's tutor in the early days at Cecil House, and who became Professor of Civil Law at Cambridge and later her Majesty's Ambassador to France; Sir John Cheke, later chief tutor to the young Prince Edward; Matthew Parker, the somewhat recalcitrant Archbishop of Canterbury; Roger Ascham, tutor to both Prince Edward and the Princess Elizabeth, and then Latin Secretary to Edward VI, Queen Mary, and Queen Elizabeth; and Sir Nicholas Bacon, Lord

111

Chancellor under Queen Elizabeth, who was also Cecil's brother-in-law.

At sixteen, Cecil lectured on logic; at eighteen, he lectured on the Greek language, both feats considered rare at the time. At twenty-two he graduated from Gray's Inn, and married Mary Cheke, sister of his classmate, John; she died a year later, leaving one son, Thomas.

William Cecil's career at Court came about almost by accident, though knowing young William as we do, we are led to believe that it might have been a carefully planned accident. He happened to be at Court to see his father, who, as we have said, was Master of the Robes to Henry VIII. While there he fell into conversation with two Irish priests in the train of their chieftain, O'Neil. They were astonished by the erudition of this young man who could discourse upon the papacy more learnedly than they themselves. The conversation was reported to the King, who promptly sent for William, took him into his service and appointed him *Custos Brevium* of the Court of Common Pleas. Possibly his early career at Court was furthered by the fact that his college friend and brother-in-law was superintending the education of the young heir apparent, Prince Edward.

In 1545 Cecil married Mildred Coke, one of the five brilliant daughters of Sir Anthony Coke, or Cooke, another tutor to the royal children of Henry VIII. What Sir Anthony taught his royal pupils by day, he relayed to his own children by evening, insisting that his daughters learn to be proficient not only in the classics, but also in such wifely pursuits as cookery and needlework.

On the accession of Edward VI, Cecil was appointed that monarch's Secretary of State. He was only twenty-eight years old, the youngest Secretary of State until that time. Then followed several years of both friendship and opposition to Somerset, and even a three months' confinement in the Tower. But upon his release, Edward VI knighted him, which showed that the young King held no animosity against him. Cecil succeeded his father as Master of the Robes, then was created Chancellor and was awarded the Order of the Garter.

When Edward lay dying, Northumberland tried to force Sir William, as Lord Chancellor, to declare Mary Tudor illegitimate, so that *his* son, Guildford Dudley, married to the Lady Jane Grey, might eventually be King. Cecil not only refused to declare Mary illegitimate, but he was unalterably opposed to the marriage of Guildford and the unlucky little Lady Jane. This may be why the new Queen, Mary Tudor, asked him to serve as her Secretary of State. Sir William declined when he realized that he would be expected to join her church. He retired to his estate at Burghley but was persuaded to be an M.P. for Stamford. It was about this time that he began to cultivate the interests and good will of the Princess Elizabeth, whose measure he had taken while serving at her brother's Court.

Correspondence between Cecil and the princess was necessarily clandestine, and extremely dangerous, since if Mary suspected it, the price would have been high for each of them. But certain it is that Cecil realized that Mary's health was failing and that before long her all-English sister would come to the throne. And most important of all to Sir William, the Princess Elizabeth was a Protestant.

It is supposed that Sir William was the first to announce Mary's death to the young Elizabeth, then living quietly at her own house, Hatfield. He is also supposed to have drafted for her her speech of acceptance to the deputation sent by the Council to announce that she was Queen. Certain it is that he was the first person sworn in to her Privy Council, again at Hatfield, and that Elizabeth said to him:

"This judgment I have of you, that you will not be corrupted with any manner of gift, and that you will be faithful to the State, and that without respect to my private will you will give me that counsel that you think best."

On Elizabeth's accession, Sir William's first attention was given to the Church, which was in a precarious state after the Catholic reign of Mary. His next concern was for the fiscal condition of the kingdom since English finances had depreciated in the last two reigns. By frugal policies and sound economic devices he was able to stabilize the currency.

In 1561 he was appointed Master of the Wards, a lucrative post. Camden tells us:

He managed this place as he did all his other, very providently for the service of his prince and the wards, for his own profit moderately, and for the benefit and advantage of his followers and retainers beneficially; yet without offence, and with great commendation for his integrity.

It is interesting that in contrast to Oxford, who had inherited great wealth but was forced to sell many of his estates to pay his debts, Lord Burghley had little when he became Secretary to the Queen, but left more than three hundred estates when he died.

Praise and appreciation were now pouring in upon Sir William, especially from his grateful sovereign, who created him Baron of Burghleigh in 1570. (He himself changed the spelling to the simpler Burghley.) The letters patent for the title tell us that he was "not advanced for his wealth, but for his worth."

In 1573 he was appointed Lord High Treasurer of England, a post he held the rest of his life. And meanwhile, his duties of Secretary were filled by his old friend, Sir Thomas Smith.

Lord Burghley entertained the Queen with a host of retainers no less than twelve times at Theobalds, "the Queen lying there at his Lordship's charge, sometimes three weeks, a month, yea, six weeks together." Indeed, Elizabeth enjoyed his hospitality at Theobalds so much that she received her ambassadors there—an honor of very great expense to her kindly and generous host. And frequently she dined with him at Cecil House on the Strand.

On one of her visits to Burghley, the Queen was forced to leave hastily because the Lady Anne Cecil had come down with smallpox.

Lord Burghley's contribution to education was no less than his contribution to state affairs. As Chancellor of the University of Cambridge, he not only adjudicated all manner of disputes between the colleges, but initiated a number of new programs. Although he founded no colleges or schools himself, he persuaded the Queen to found Trinity College, Dublin, in 1591, and he himself drew up the plan of studies to be pursued there. Both Lord Burghley and his illustrious wife, the Lady Mildred, founded scholarships in schools and colleges.

Yet he was a curious person, this eminent statesman, and we confess to much sympathy for his son-in-law, Edward. That great mind which in the long reign of

Queen Elizabeth had focussed on the delicate intricacies of church affairs, the precarious implications of foreign policy, the stabilization of the currency, the possibilities inherent in the Queen's marriage, the placating of a recalcitrant Parliament, the involved matters of the succession, the intra-college feuds of Cambridge University, the intrigue of foreign spies, and a thousand other matters pertaining to the welfare of the kingdom—this mind could so methodically concern itself with minutiae that he bought some scales and weighed in each member of his family, including himself, then weighed each member of his household staff, noting the results in a pocket memorandum! He even made an inventory of his clothes!

The advice he gave his son, good enough in its way, is ridiculed in *Hamlet* by Polonius' prosaic instructions to *his* son. Indeed, Lord Burghley seems to have been the butt of mischievous satire on the part of the younger courtiers, egged on, no doubt, by the former Royal Ward, the Earl of Oxford. Here is a typical homily of Burghley's:

> The quickest way to do many things is to do only one thing at a time.

(Edward, we imagine, was usually trying to do twenty things at once.)

Lord Burghley's complete lack of humor is shown in the following letter [1] from him to Sir Francis Walsingham, dated August 10, 1586, complaining about the constabulary:

> Sir—As I cam from London homward, in my

_____

1. This letter with its original spelling is taken from the notes to *Much Ado About Nothing,* in the Yale Shakespeare, edited by Tucker Brooke.

coche, I sawe at euery townes end the nombre of x. or xij. standying, with long staues, and vntill I came to Enfield I thought no other of them, but that they had stayed for auodying of the rayne, or to drynk at some alehouses, for so they did stand vnder pentices (penthouses) at alehouses. But at Enfield fynding a dosen in a plump (group), whan ther was no rayne, I bethought myself that they was apoynted as watchmen, for the apprehendying of such as are missying, (i.e. certain escaped traitors); and thereupon I called some of them to me apart, and asked them wherfor they stood ther? And on of them answered,—To take 3 yong men. And demandying how they shuld know the persons, on answered with these words: Marry, my Lord, by intelligence of ther fauor. What means you by that? quoth I. Marry, sayd they, on of the partyes hath a hooked nose.—And haue you, quoth I, no other mark?—No, sayth they. And then I asked who apoynted them; and they answered on Bankes, a Head Constable, whom I willed to be sent to me.— Suerly, sir, who so euer had the chardg from you hath vsed the matter negligently, for these watchmen stand so oppenly in plumps, as no suspected person will come neare them; and if they be no better instructed but to fynd 3 persons by on of them hauying a hooked nose, they may miss thereof. And thus I thought good to aduertise yow, that the Justyces that had the chardg. as I thynk, may vse the matter more circumspectly.

Yet in this great man there are homely little touches which are both amusing and endearing. He wrote in his diary, for instance, that on retiring for the night, he would put off his robes of state and looking upon them, would say: "Lye there, Lord Treasurer," and then fall fast asleep.

117

Though not always did he sleep so soundly. His secretary tells us:

> I have heard him say, he did penetrate further into the depth of causes and found out more resolution of dubious points in his bed than when he was up. Indeed, he left himself scarce time for sleep, or meals, or leisure, and his Prince and country were so pleased he thought his pains a pleasure. . . . So great was his care and love to his Prince and country.

From time to time we have referred to the relations between Lord Burghley and his son-in-law, Oxford, and vice versa. In this biography we do not subscribe to the theory that Burghley frankly detested Lord Oxford after his faithlessness to Anne, because we have too many existing records to prove that each man made the effort to be friendly and considerate of the other. This does not mean, however, that Burghley ever forgave Edward the disgrace and humiliation he had caused Anne.

Also, Edward's extravagances and thriftlessness must have been exasperating to the older man, especially since in later years it was clearly his duty to try to save some of the Oxford estates for his three granddaughters.

Edward on his part seems to have tried to be respectful and pleasing to his father-in-law. Soon after his marriage he wrote to Burghley that he "desires your Lordship to pardon my youth, but to take in good part my zeal and affection towards you."

In 1590, when Burghley was old and infirm and grieving over the loss of his wife and daughter, we find that Edward, aged forty, writes of him with gratitude and pathos:

who in all my causes I find mine honourable good
Lord, and to deal more fatherly than friendly with
me, the which I do acknowledge—and ever will—
myself in the special wise bound.

Lord Burghley suffered greatly with his gout and his
stomach trouble toward the end of his life. Yet each day
he ordered his coach and drove out through the teeming
streets of London to the nearby countryside to take the
air.

There is a touching story that in his last illness the
Queen went to Cecil House, sat by his bedside and fed
him with her own hand. She called him not only her
Treasurer but her dearest treasure. And when he died
she wept tears of grief. Indeed, for several years after,
whenever he was mentioned, she wept quietly.

Lord Burghley died in 1598. Though he was buried
in Stamford, there was a simultaneous funeral for him in
Westminster Abbey. An empty coffin covered with a purple
pall rested in the choir six days. The seventh day the
funeral service was held, with music by the Queen's
own choristers.

Lord Burghley left two sons: Thomas, the child of his
first wife, who became the Earl of Exeter; and Robert,
the hunchback, who tried so hard to fill his father's place
as Secretary to the Queen. He was later created Marquess
of Salisbury by James I. Besides Anne, Countess of Oxford, who had died ten years before, Burghley had another
daughter, Elizabeth, a goddaughter to the Queen, who
later married William Wentworth.

No two people appreciated each other more than did
Queen Elizabeth and her faithful servant, William Cecil.
Of him she might have said, as was said of Caesar:

I have not known when his affections swayed
More than his reason.

Meanwhile, Lord Burghley had written this estimate of his Queen:

She had so rare gifts, as when her Council had said all they could, she would find out a wise counsel beyond all theirs.

Chapter XV

THE QUEEN: 1600

"Long live, long live fair Oriana!"
Elizabethan Madrigal.

Undoubtedly the person who had the greatest influence upon Edward's life was the Queen. All-powerful, she it was who exercised her prerogative in determining his coming and his going, his leaving the country and his return, his attendance at Court and his free time for private living and writing. She had power over his written word, as he records sadly in Sonnet 66: ". . . and art made tongue-tied by authority." She even had power over his religious thought, forcing him to renounce Catholicism, remembered in the same sonnet: ". . . purest faith unhappily forsworn."

She came into our story a beautiful young woman of twenty-eight with golden hair, bright eyes and a fresh complexion. Now, in the year 1600, she is old at sixty-seven with a red wig, ghastly white-painted face, long blackened teeth, high domineering nose and deep-set, piercing eyes. Perhaps it is her mouth that is most noticeable in the portraits of this time—that peevish, stubborn mouth. Her hands are wrinkled now, the long tapering fingers laden with jewelled rings; but still she uses them gracefully when she talks. She stoops a little. But there is about her a queenly aura. She is more regal than when she had her beauty.

In 1558 Elizabeth had come to the throne of a small island kingdom riddled with dissension in church and in state, surrounded by covetous nations. With the advice of her chosen ministers, but even more by the wisdom and force of her own compelling personality, she had made England one of the great powers of the age. Proud and patriotic her people were, and worshipfully in love with her, their sovereign. This passage in *King Richard II* reflects that pride and patriotism:

> This royal throne of kings, this scepter'd isle,
> This earth of majesty, this seat of Mars,
> This other Eden, demi-paradise,
> This fortress built by Nature for herself
> Against infection and the hand of war,
> This happy breed of men, this little world,
> This precious stone set in the silver sea,
> Which serves it in the office of a wall,
> Or as a moat defensive to a house,
> Against the envy of less happier lands,
> This blessed plot, this earth, this realm, this England.
>   (Act II, sc. 1.)

By her own brand of feminine diplomacy Elizabeth had kept the peace with France and Spain. By her courage and her eloquence she had stirred her people to defeat the mighty Spanish Armada. By her devious means, as well as by her drastic imprisonments and executions, she had kept the Catholics at bay. True, Spain was still at war in the Low Countries, and the war with Ireland was not yet won. But to the old Queen, Tyrone was only a buzzing gnat on a sultry day, and her current favorite, Robin Devereux, would soon dispose of him.

Within her own borders, England was at peace. And during Queen Elizabeth's reign, learning had progressed in schools and colleges, the arts had flourished, and the known world had widened to include lands and riches undreamed of before she came to the throne.

Of special interest to us is her encouragement of the drama. One remarkable aspect of her reign is not only that there were so many dramatists, but that they were able to produce so many plays. This is all the more noteworthy because the Puritan influence was being turned against theatres and playwrights, and there was a perpetual cold war between the theatre managers and the London Council, which tried again and again to close down the playhouses. In 1592 they were closed because of the plague, and it was with the greatest difficulty that they were opened again in June of 1594, the Puritans trying to use the plague orders to keep them shut.

"Whosoever shall visit the chapel of Satan," writes one of the sixteenth century Puritans of London, "I mean the Theatre, shall find there no want of young ruffians."

Another writes of the manners of the London apprentices:

"Many by nature honest and tractable, have been altered by these shows and spectacles and become monstrous."

But a preacher at Paul's Cross gives the real reason the Puritans protested so vehemently against the theatres:

"Will not a filthy play, with a blast of trumpets," he demands, "sooner call thither a thousand than an hour's tolling of a bell bring to the sermon a hundred?"

When the protests became too urgent, the theatre managers appealed to the Queen, who, invariably on their side, decreed that the theatres stay open. All her life Elizabeth had enjoyed dramatics. How she would appreciate the grandeur of the Shakespearean historical plays, the subtle compliments to herself and her forbears, the lilt and rhythm of the lines! Rumor has it that she laughed so hard at Falstaff in *King Henry the Fourth* that she commanded the playwright to do another play about the fat knight in love. He obliged by writing *Merry Wives of Windsor* in fourteen days.

There is a charming painting of the Queen being carried in state to the Blackfriars in 1596. Of course she did not go to the public theatres, but the Blackfriars was in a sense private.

For Queen Elizabeth's championship of the drama we owe her an incalculable debt of gratitude. Without her encouragement we should have no Hamlet, no Lear, no Cleopatra, no Macbeth.

Elizabeth, the woman, has fascinated biographers for four centuries. Although age did wither her unmercifully, custom could not stale her infinite variety, and the contradictions in her character are part of her undying charm. Queenly she was, yet at times she had the manners of a fishwife. Generous she could be, yet she was parsimonious to her soldiers fighting England's wars. Lavish in praise when the spirit moved her, she could drain the blood from the face of the proudest courtier by her high-pitched, rasping abuse. With foreign emissaries she could discourse most learnedly in Latin, French or Italian, yet she could write a letter of condolence in simple, moving English words to one of the meanest of her subjects who had lost a son in the war. She would brook no fancy airs from her aspiring courtiers—("God's Son! I am no Queen; that man is above me!" she exclaimed of Essex)—yet she could so sympathize with a stumbling orator in the country that she told him his address was the finest she had ever heard.

Throughout her long life there filed before her a procession of favorites, beginning with the Earl of Leicester, who was probably the only man she ever really loved. Then followed Sir Christopher Hatton, Sir Christopher Blount, Sir Walter Raleigh, Sir Philip Sidney, Edward de Vere, Earl of Oxford, and now Robert Devereux, the glamorous young Earl of Essex, stepson of her first love. Gallant, handsome, charming young men, each had caught her fancy, then been eclipsed by a younger man. Elizabeth was a born coquette, and her feminine ego demanded the presence of an adoring flatterer kneeling at her feet, as respite from affairs of state. Yet each one of them had felt the sting of her tongue at one time or another.

"Go home!" she screamed at her godson, Sir John Harington. And he writes: "I did not stay to be bidden twice. If all the Irish rebels had been at my heels, I should not have had better speed."

Most of these chivalrous young courtiers exerted the attraction of opposites. Few of them were her intellectual equals. But Edward de Vere seems to have been almost her masculine counterpart—brilliant, emotional, impetuous, volatile, unpredictable. Between them, the Queen and Oxford, there was that mysterious magnetism that in the days of their youth had attracted and repelled and attracted them to one another again. The jealous Elizabeth Tudor doubtless would never forgive Edward for his affair with Anne Vavasor. Yet we have reason to believe that as the years wore on, a friendship ripened between

125

the Queen and her courtier based on loyalty and mutual respect. Edward would always appreciate Elizabeth's queenly grace—her grace of mind and grace of spirit—while her Majesty, we may be sure, was ever attracted by Edward's intellect and his charm. Moreover, Elizabeth trusted him, trusted his judgment. Toward the end of her life there were not many of whom she could be so sure.

In an Elizabethan anthology there is a little poem signed "The E. of Ox.," but the same poem in the Rawlinson manuscript is attributed to the Queen. Did the great Queen deign so to open her heart that she was willing to allow her quill pen to give away her most secret emotions? Or was Edward, Earl of Oxford, so sympathetic to that pulsating heart of hers that he knew her better than she knew herself? These are teasing questions. Here is the poem: [1]

> When I was fair and young then favour gracèd me;
> Of many I was sought their mistress for to be.
> But I did scorn them all, and answered them therefore,
> Go, go, go, seek some otherwhere,
>   Importune me no more.
>
> How many weeping eyes I made to pine in woe;
> How many sighing hearts I have no skill to show;
> Yet I the prouder grew, and answered them therefore,
> Go, go, go, seek some otherwhere,
>   Importune me no more.
>
> Then spake fair Venus' son, that proud victorious boy,
> And said, you dainty dame, since that you be so coy,

---

1. From *The Spenser Anthology*, edited by Edward Alber, London, 1901.

I will so pluck your plumes that you shall say no more,
Go, go, go, seek some otherwhere,
                    Importune me no more.

When he spake these words such change grew in my breast,
That neither night or day I could take any rest.
Then lo! I did repent, that I had said before
Go, go, go, seek some otherwhere,
                    Importune me no more.[2]

---

2. Cf. st. 2, line 2, with *Lucrece,* st. 12, line 4:
    Which far exceeds his barren skill to show.
Cf. again the repeated refrain with *Two Gentlemen of Verona,* Act
V, sc. 4, line 40:
    Therefore be gone, solicit me no more.
Note: The Ogburns write: "This poem signed by Oxford and attributed to Elizabeth might be the 'letter' Valentine and Silvia are talking about in the rather cryptic scene in *Two Gentlemen,* Act II,
sc. 1, lines 108-9, which rhymes *discover* and *lover* after the manner
of the *Echo poems*

Or fearing else some messenger that might her mind discover
Herself hath taught her love himself to write unto her lover."

Chapter XVI

THE TRIAL OF ESSEX AND SOUTHAMPTON

> "So we'll live,
> And pray, and sing, and tell old tales, and laugh
> At gilded butterflies, and hear poor rogues
> Talk of court news; and we'll talk with them too:
> Who loses and who wins, who's in, who's out;
> And take upon's the mystery of things,
> As if we were God's spies."
>
> *King Lear.*

Meanwhile, Edward was not completely retired from public life. We find that in 1601 he was summoned with twenty-four other noblemen to sit on a Commission of Peers, called to try the Earls of Essex and Southampton, accused of treason. That Oxford was chosen to be the presiding lord is proof once again that the Queen and Court depended upon his authority, his prestige and his ability.

Court honors and Court privileges had turned the head of the handsome, blueblooded Earl of Essex. He had been presented to the Queen by his stepfather, the Earl of Leicester, who, as Sir Robert Dudley, we met at the beginning of this story when Dudley was the reigning favorite at Court. Since then, as we have learned, other young men have knelt at the feet of the Queen, including Edward himself, while Leicester, his glamour tarnished by gray hair and a bulging figure, waited in the offing. He sought to curry favor once again by introducing his tall and gallant stepson.

From his first day in attendance the young man was a success at Court. Among his comrades there was the young Earl of Southampton, who had been brought up with Essex in Lord Burghley's gracious mansion on the Strand when both were Royal Wards. Robert Devereux, Earl of Essex, like Oxford, belonged to the old aristocracy; he inherited the blood of Plantagenet kings, in contrast to Wriothesley, who was only the *Third* Earl of Southampton. Moreover, Essex was a cousin of the Queen through her mother, Anne Boleyn.

Leicester's plan worked better than he had anticipated. To use the words of King Lear in quite another sense, "The wheel is come full circle." The young man Elizabeth first loved, was reincarnated and once again kneeling at her feet. The Queen saw in Essex a repetition of her early romance with Leicester.

That aging earl soon found that it was unnecessary to push forward his young stepson. The tall, auburn-haired youth with the boyish spirits was never separated from the Queen. There were long talks in the Privy Apartments at Whitehall, long walks in the garden and fruit orchards, long rides in the parks and woods around London, long lazy afternoons on the river in that month of

129

May, 1587. In the evening there were more talks, more laughter and music—until at last the great palace was quiet and empty of its glittering courtiers—empty except for these two, the Queen and the Earl playing cards together—cards or other games, so that a gossip at the palace tells us "my Lord cometh not to his own lodging till birds sing in the morning."

The Queen was fifty-three, the Earl not yet twenty. "It was a dangerous concatenation of ages," writes Lytton Strachey. Yet in that May and June all was well. Strachey continues:

> If only time could have stood still for a little and drawn out those halcyon weeks through vague ages of summer! The boy, in his excitement, walking home through the dawn, the smiling Queen in the darkness . . . but there is no respite for mortal creatures. Human relationships must either move or perish. When two consciousnesses come to a certain nearness and the impetus of their interactions, growing ever intenser and intenser, leads on to an inescapable climax, the crescendo must rise to its topmost note; and only then is the preordained solution of the theme made manifest.

How well the great playwright also understood these truths! He has drawn his own impression of the fall of Essex in one of the last of his plays, *Coriolanus*. There is no detailed resemblance between the Roman general and the English earl; indeed, there are many variances. For instance, Coriolanus despised the plebeians of Rome, whereas Essex deliberately courted the people of London. The similarity lies in the fact that each leader was proud and irritable, always chafing against imposed restriction and limitation. Each leader was the agent of his own ruin.

You might have been enough the man you are,
With striving less to be so . . .

This phrase describes Coriolanus, but no less it is applicable to Essex. Again, an old enemy speaks thus of Coriolanus after he defected to the Volscians and planned the attack on Rome:

> I think he'll be to Rome
> As is the osprey to the fish, who takes it
> By sovereignty of nature. First he was
> A noble servant to them, but he could not
> Carry his honours even. Whether 'twas pride,
> Which out of daily fortune ever taints
> The happy man; whether defect of judgment,
> To fail in the disposing of those chances
> Which he was lord of . . .

Essex surely lacked judgment. Nor could he "carry his honours even." These were the reasons for his downfall.

But this is Oxford's story, and the career of the younger earl can be outlined only briefly here.

The ominous troubles with Spain were drawing to a head. Essex demanded permission to fight in Cadiz. This was granted, though reluctantly, by the Queen, and Essex set forth with Southampton by his side. While in Cadiz he distinguished himself for bravery in action, if not for military competence. Returning to London, he had his portrait painted with the beard he had nurtured in Cadiz. This remarkably lifelike painting is now in the National Portrait Gallery.

The arrogant earl, still Court favorite, spent the next months attending on the Queen in a sort of dilatory fashion and a great deal more time philandering with the Ladies in Waiting. He was known to have had a child by Mistress Elizabeth Southwell, and gossip linked his name also with Lady Mary Howard and Mistress Russell—all of which was disquieting not only to the Queen but to the Countess, his wife.

The truth was that, like other courtiers we have met, Essex was chafing at the restrictions of Court life and longing for further military glory. Finally he prevailed upon the Queen to place him in command of the English forces in Ireland, as her Lord Deputy, fighting against Tyrone, a formidable foe. And by his side again was Southampton.

It was during this phase of the Irish Campaign that *King Henry V* was playing at the Globe Theatre to great applause from "the groundlings." The playwright, mindful of the appeal of current history as well as the popularity of Essex with the London people, alludes to him in the speech of the *Chorus* describing the victorious return of King Henry from the Battle of Agincourt:

> But now behold
> In the quick forge and working-house of thought,
> How London doth pour out her citizens!
> The mayor, and all his brethren, in best sort,—
> Like to the senators of antique Rome,
> With the plebeians swarming at their heels—
> Go forth, and fetch their conquering Caesar in:
> As, by lower but loving likelihood,
> Were now the general of our gracious empress
> (As in good time, he may) from Ireland coming,
> Bringing rebellion broached on his sword,
> How many would the peaceful city quit
> To welcome him!

This passage would surely be applauded in the theatre, for many times had these same Londoners seen the handsome earl riding by the side of their Queen.

But the playwright's prophecy did not come true. Actually, the Irish campaign did not succeed under the command of Essex. His arrogance and incompetence, not to say plain laziness, angered the Queen so much that she did not support him fully with arms and men. He got sick in Dublin, and from his couch he wrote her this letter, in which he betrays more jealousy than fidelity:

> But why do I talk of victory or success? Is it not known that from England I receive nothing but disconsolate comfort and soul's wounds? Is it not spoken in the army, that your Majesty's favour is diverted from me? . . . Is it not lamented of your Majesty's faithfullest subjects, both there and here, that . . . a Raleigh— I will forbear other for their places' sakes—should have such credit and success with your Majesty when they wish the ill-success of your Majesty's faithfullest servant.

But still he procrastinated. A Court gossip wrote:

> Essex hath done so little; he tarries yet in Dublin.

The climax came when he used his powers as Lord Deputy to create no less than fifty-nine knights, and, most aggravating of all, made Southampton his Master of Horse.

Angrily the Queen demanded that he retract the last honor immediately. Southampton was recalled to London, if not in actual disgrace, at least without honor.

Meanwhile there was the problem of how to handle

Essex. The Queen sought advice from a curious quarter. One day at Nonesuch she met Sir Francis Bacon walking in the garden. Bacon, with his brother, Anthony, had belonged to the Essex clique. The Queen approached him. Knowing him to be a clever man, she said, she wondered if perhaps she could extract from him some words of wisdom which might help her in dealing with my Lord Essex. This is his reply:

Madam, if you had my Lord of Essex here with a white staff in his hand, as my Lord of Leicester had, and continued him still about you for society to yourself, and for an honour and ornament to your attendance and Court in the eyes of your people, and in the eyes of foreign ambassadors, then were he in his right element. For to discontent him as you do, and yet to put arms and power into his hands, may be a kind of temptation to make him prove cumbersome and unruly. And therefore if you would send for him, and satisfy him with honour here near you, if your affairs—which I am not acquainted with—will permit it, I think it were the best way.

The Queen thanked him and passed on. She pondered long upon his advice, but she did not heed it.

Instead, she sent orders to Essex to stay in Ireland until Tyrone was dispatched. But the impetuous earl disobeyed her Majesty's command and returned to London. Then he enraged her by crashing into her boudoir unannounced. That was the final insult to the Queen; Essex had seen her without her wig!

She delayed long enough to cool her temper before deciding what course to pursue. Then the Queen gave orders that Essex was to be taken into custody. He was confined first at York House in the care of Lord Bacon, and later in his own great palace of Essex House on the Strand around the bend in the river from Whitehall.

Meanwhile the secret service found that for eighteen months Essex had been carrying on an intriguing correspondence with King James of Scotland. Yet, in spite of this incriminating discovery, when he came to his own house, his guard was relaxed. Essex, with his band of insurgents, including Southampton, began to lay plans.

On Saturday, February seventh of that year, 1601, the Lord Chamberlain's Company performed the play, *Richard II*, at the insistent demand of Sir Charles Percy, one of Essex's henchmen. The players gave every excuse to avoid presenting this inflammatory drama at such a time of tension, telling Sir Charles that the play was out of date and that they couldn't afford to produce it for the small audience it might draw. Whereupon Sir Charles offered the actors an outright sum of 40 shillings, which the Chamberlain's Company finally accepted. Essex and his party dined at Gunter's and were then rowed across the river to the Globe to see the play of the "killing of Richard the second." To the relief of the players the production caused no unruly disturbance.

Sunday morning, February 8th, Essex impetuously decided to lead his followers in a march on the City. It is not clear what he expected to accomplish but he must have thought that this time he could arouse the citizenry to follow him. He knew well that he had been their darling, knew with what admiration they had gazed up at him when he used to ride so proudly with the Queen.

With Sir Christopher Blount leading, they set out

with a slender band of scarce two hundred, that fateful
Sunday morning, their swords wrapped in their cloaks,
walking at a brisk pace up the Strand to Fleet Street crying: "Saw! Saw! Saw! Tray! Tray!" Charging up Ludgate
Hill they arrived just as the congregation were filing out
of church. . . . But the expected uprising did not occur.
The citizens of London were ever loyal to their Sovereign
Lady, Queen Elizabeth, no matter what dashing young
courtier might attempt to win them over to insurrection.
Ignominiously Essex fled to the river where he found a
boat moored and rowed himself home to the Water Gate
of Essex House. While he was hurriedly burning his incriminating papers the Queen's troops arrived with ar-
tillery. Essex gave himself up and was taken to the Tower.

The Earl of Southampton's implication in the thwarted
uprising seems to have been only as an accomplice; yet
he, too, as one of the Essex group, was confined in the
Tower. More than a hundred persons were taken to prison
and interrogated by the Crown authorities.

The Queen decreed that the two noble earls, Essex
and Southampton, should be tried separately from the
other prisoners, by the special Commission of Peers of
which the Earl of Oxford would be the presiding officer.

The trial [1] was held in Westminster Hall, February
18th. Essex and Southampton arrived early. Essex, dressed
all in black, gazed disdainfully upon the gathering assem-
bly. When Lord Grey—a former enemy at Court—was
sworn in as one of the twenty-four judges, Essex "laughed
upon" Southampton and pulled his sleeve. And as the
indictment was read, he smiled benignly, lifting his eyes

---

1. This description of the trial is a very brief summary of the
dramatic account given in Lytton Strachey's *Elizabeth and Essex*.

to the carved oak ceiling of Westminster Hall in mocking wonder.

Actually, the trial was a strange proceeding staged by those law-loving Elizabethans, the result being a foregone conclusion. The Court of Peers had consulted the learned judges of the City beforehand, who gave their opinion that, whatever had been the intention of Essex and his followers, their March on the City constituted treason and sentence must be passed. For some reason, doubtless for fear of the ideas that might be suggested to other would-be insurgents, it had been decided beforehand that Essex's intrigue with James of Scotland should be ignored. So the case hung on that Sunday march. The accused were allowed no counsel, their right of cross-examination was cut to the minimum, and evidence of the witnesses was read aloud to the court in the form of depositions extracted from prisoners in the Tower. Sir Edward Coke, prosecutor for the Crown, soon won sympathy for the defendants by his rough and abusive treatment of them. During the wranglings, Essex confused the issues by interrupting to bring up a number of irrelevant matters. He declared that Sir Walter Raleigh intended to murder him, which Raleigh forthwith denied.

Essex then accused Sir Robert Cecil, the Queen's Secretary and Oxford's brother-in-law, of conniving with Spain in regard to the succession. This charge provoked a moment of intense dramatic effect. For Cecil, who had been listening to the trial from behind a curtain, suddenly stepped out and falling on his knees, begged the court to allow him to clear himself of the slander. Permission was granted and, after considerable argument with Essex, Cecil managed to elicit the information that the young earl had learned of the suspected intrigue from his uncle,

Sir William Knollys. Knollys was then sent for and, of course, repudiated his nephew's charge. So the Secretary was absolved, and retired behind his curtain.[2]

Hours later the prosecution had come no nearer proof of criminal intent on the part of the two earls, and Coke was shaking his finger at Essex, shouting: "It was your purpose to take not only the Tower of London but the royal palace and the person of the prince—yea, and to take away her life!"

At this point Lord Bacon took over the prosecution. Addressing his learned Peers, he compared the Essex March on London with Pisistratus' March on Athens, when "he went crying into the streets that his life was sought and like to be taken away."

Later Bacon compared the march again with an incident from more recent history, the uprising in Paris when the Duc de Guise had stirred up the populace against Henri III. This proved to be a master stroke, and was not lost upon Cecil, the Secretary, still hiding behind the curtain.

Both prisoners were found guilty and sentence was passed. The Earl of Essex was condemned to death, but Southampton escaped with imprisonment in the Tower.

The trial lasted eleven hours. It must have been a long and tiring ordeal for Oxford to sit through as Presiding Officer. Essex had been bold, petulant and intransigent. But we may imagine that it was not Essex, but his accomplice, Southampton, whose fate more nearly concerned the aristocratic judge. What memories had been evoked that cold February day in Westminster Hall, as Edward went back in his mind to the beginning of their friendship so

---

2. We are reminded of the scene in *Hamlet* in which Polonius is found hiding "behind the arras" in the queen's chamber.

long ago, their attendance at Court together, their rivalry for Anne Vavasor's favors, and the betrothal to Elizabeth de Vere, which Southampton had so peremptorily broken off!

The Earl of Essex was executed on Tower Green; he was not yet thirty-five years old. Southampton remained a prisoner in the Tower, "where he languished sulkily and had his portrait painted with his favorite cat." [3]

Upon the accession of the new king, Southampton was pardoned and set free through the intervention of the Earl of Oxford.

<hr>

3. Quoted from Peter Quennell, *Shakespeare, a Biography.*

Chapter XVII

LAST YEARS OF THE QUEEN AND
HER COURTIER

"Time's thievish progress to eternity."
Sonnet 77.

There was one more occasion when Oxford had the honor of serving as courtier to the Queen. That was in October of 1601, when Elizabeth summoned her last Parliament. There had been dissatisfaction over the monopolies—those grants of the sole right to sell certain goods and articles. The Queen used these grants to reward her favorites; for instance, both Leicester and Essex had had the monopoly of the sweet wines. In 1595 the Earl of Oxford and Lord Buckhurst eagerly bid against each other for the monopoly of tin, but it finally went to Sir Walter Raleigh.

By 1601 the monopolies had become a stormy issue in the House of Commons. Elizabeth decided to go direct to

Parliament herself to discuss the matter. She went in state, as always. But as she stood in her heavy robes of office before the Lords and Commons, she tottered and would have fallen had not several gentlemen reached forward to support her.

Protests on the monopolies began. She listened and realized the discontent the system had aroused. She withdrew and sent for the Speaker. She told him she was aware that "divers patents, which she had granted, were grievous to her subjects," and promised immediate reform.

When the Commons heard what had happened, their discontent was turned to overwhelming loyalty. In a wave of gratitude and admiration, they sent a deputation, who assured her that "in all duty and thankfulness, prostrate at your feet we present our most loyal and thankful hearts."

The Queen then asked permission to address the Commons. Every knee bowed as she appeared.

"There is no jewel," she began, "be it of never so rich a price, which I prefer before this jewel, I mean your love. For I do more esteem it than any treasure or riches; for that we know how to prize, but love and thanks I count inestimable. And though God hath raised me high, yet this I count the glory of my crown, that I have reigned with your loves. This makes that I do not so much rejoice that God hath made me a Queen, as to be Queen over so thankful a people."

She paused, and bade them stand, as she had more to say. Then gesturing gracefully with her hands, she thanked the House for bringing their grievances to her, as otherwise she might have erred through lack of information. She said she had never made any grant except in belief that it was beneficial; she was glad to know if experience proved it otherwise.

141

"I do appeal," she continued, "that never thought was cherished in my heart that tended not to my people's good."

She then proceeded with these eloquent words:

"To be a King and wear a crown is more glorious to them that see it than it is pleasure to them that bear it. For myself I was never so much enticed with the glorious name of a King, or royal authority of a Queen, as delighted that God hath made me the instrument to maintain His Truth and Glory, and to defend the kingdom from peril, dishonour, tyranny and oppression. There will never Queen sit in my seat with more zeal to my country, or care to my subjects, that will sooner with willingness yield and venture her life for your good and safety than myself. And though you had, and may have, many princes more mighty and wise sitting in this seat, yet you never had, nor shall have, any that will be more careful and loving."

The Queen stopped speaking. There was a pregnant pause, then a sound of trumpets. Straightening herself, the Queen swept from the hall with her attendants. Never had she been so regal! Never had she been so endearing!

There is one very small incident of her last years which must be recorded here because it concerns people we have met before. The Queen used to enjoy making fun of Sir Robert Cecil, the little hunchback Secretary who tried so awkwardly to pay his court to her.

One day the Queen saw the Countess of Derby, our friend, Elizabeth de Vere, wearing a picture-locket and asked to see it. The Countess demurred, but the Queen insisted. The picture proved to be of Cecil, Elizabeth de Vere's uncle.

The Queen thereupon took the locket and tied it to

her shoe and walked away. Later she fastened it to her elbow and wore it that way for some time.

Cecil wrote a poem about the incident and had it set to music and sung to his Royal Mistress.

The sands of time were running out for both the Queen and her courtier, Oxford. Actually, they were growing old—old for their time, and old considering the lives they had spent. Each had lived fully, often dangerously, though neither had known the fulfillment of the dreams of youth.

It was the rebellion and trial of Essex and Southampton which had aged them both, even more than the passing years. For each it had been a bitter disillusionment, a betrayal of what had been more than a friendship—between the Queen and Essex, between Oxford and Southampton.

Yet how different were the lives of the Queen and her courtier at this time! Oxford was enjoying the quiet comfort of a contented home with his young and beautiful Countess Elizabeth and their son, Henry de Vere, Viscount Bolebec, at Hackney. By this time there were grandchildren to be brought out to King's Place from time to time to give the doting grandfather a glimpse into the future.

However, we trace a mood of sadness in Edward's sonnets of this time. This is Sonnet 65:

Since brass, nor stone, nor earth, nor boundless sea,
But sad mortality o'ersways their power,
How with this rage shall beauty hold a plea,
Whose action is no stronger than a flower?
O, how shall summer's honey breath hold out
Against the wrackfull siege of battering days,

143

When rocks impregnable are not so stout,
Nor gates of steel so strong, but Time decays?
O fearful meditation! where, alack,
Shall Time's best jewel from Time's chest lie hid?
Or what strong hand can hold his swift foot back?
Or who his spoil of beauty can forbid?
O, none, unless this miracle have might,
That in black ink my love may still shine bright.

Queen Elizabeth was quite alone amid her courtiers and Maids of Honor. Had she not always been alone? But now even more than ever. She continued to be the center of the ceremonies of the Court; indeed, she would have missed it had she not been.

The first months after Essex's death she had been bravely controlled. But now the inevitable reaction followed as the full realization of what had happened pressed in upon her consciousness. Her temper grew worse, her rages more frequent. Sometimes she would shut herself up in a dark room and weep in a paroxysm of grief. When much later she came out scowling, she would berate her serving-women for some fancied neglect until they, too, were reduced to tears.

Sir John Harington tells us she could hardly eat; only a "little manchet and succory potage" passed her lips. Most of the time she sat silent and melancholy. She kept a sword by her side, which she would suddenly snatch up, and stamping to and fro, she would finally thrust it into the tapestry.

Even Sir John, when he asked for an audience, received a rude reply:

"Go tell that witty fellow, my god-son, to get home; it is no season now to fool it here."

But another time in the winter of 1602, Sir John did obtain an audience.

"I found her," he wrote his wife, "in most pitiable state."

The Queen asked him if he had ever seen Tyrone.

"I replied with reverence," he writes, "that I had seen him with the Lord Deputy; she looked up with much choler and grief in her countenance and said, 'Oh, now it mindeth me that you was one who saw this man elsewhere,' and hereat she dropped a tear, and smote her bosom."

Sir John thought to amuse her by reading some of his rhyming epigrams, but she only smiled faintly.

"When thou dost feel creeping time at the gate," she said, "these fooleries will please thee less; I am past my relish for such matters."

However, with the Christmas revels and the festivities of the New Year of 1603, her spirits revived, and she attended some of the state dinners, and even some of the revels.

Early in the year she left the city for the country air of Richmond, the estate she loved. There, on February second, the Lord Chamberlain's Men presented a play, possibly the recently completed *Hamlet,* though this seems to be conjecture only.

Slowly but surely the Queen's strength was ebbing away with no definite symptoms but deep depression of mind. She ate and drank little, she would allow no doctors to come near her. She just sat in a low chair, brooding.

Finally it was apparent to those around her that a crisis was imminent. Struggling to rise, she fell back, then summoned her attendants to pull her to her feet. There she stood, refusing further help. The awestricken ladies watched in silence as the indomitable old woman fought her last earthly battle. She fought as she had lived, with tenacity. For fifteen hours she stood, until sheer physical weakness overcame her. Still she refused to go to bed.

She sank down on the pillows spread about her by her devoted ladies, and there she lay for four days and nights with her finger in her mouth. One of the Ladies in Waiting walking down a dark gallery to seek a little rest caught sight in the flickering candlelight of a shadowy form sweeping away, familiar in its dignity and majesty. Terrified, the lady ran back to the royal chamber—and there was the old Queen just as she had left her, lying back on the pillows with her finger in her mouth.

Finally Sir Robert Cecil was bold to say:

"Your Majesty, to content the people, you must go to bed." Then Elizabeth Tudor found her voice and strength to use it. She said:

"Little man, little man, the word *must* is not used to princes." But not long after, she yielded and was carried to bed.

She asked for music, and her Court musicians were brought in; they seemed to give her pleasure and relief. The Archbishop of Canterbury came, Whitgift, the old man whom she used to call her "little black husband." When he started to pray beside her bed, she indicated that she preferred to hear the tinkling music.

Then, unexpectedly, she seemed to find comfort in his ministrations. The poor old man prayed beside her until his old knees were in an agony of aching, but when he moved to rise, she motioned him to continue praying. He prayed on and on for what seemed to him an interminable time, until he saw that she had fallen asleep.

Sometime during the night she ceased to breathe; her

ladies beside her never knew exactly when. It was March twenty-fourth, in the year 1603.

For the last time Edward bore the canopy over her Majesty—at her funeral in Westminster Abbey. The service was a ceremony of great pomp, and there was hardly a dry eye in the Abbey, perhaps in all London.

Lord Oxford wrote to Secretary Cecil that "she hath left (me) either without sail whereby to take advantage of the prosperous gale, or without anchor to ride till the storm be overpast." But it was in *King John* that he wrote of his own heartfelt grief and never-ending loyalty to his Queen:

> Art thou gone so? I do but stay behind
> To do the office for thee . . .
> And then my soul shall wait on thee in heaven,
> As it on earth hath been, thy servant still.

Edward held the canopy once again, at the coronation of the new king, James, but he must have known that the Golden Age was over. When James was crowned, few people bothered to come to the Abbey, for London was in the grip of one of the terrible epidemics that plagued that rat-infested city, and James hurried from the Abbey to Windsor to try to escape the fever.

The year after the old Queen died, Edward himself fell ill of one of the dread infections. On June 24th, 1604, he died, in the fifty-fifth year of his life. The proud title of Eighteenth Earl fell to Elizabeth Trentham de Vere's eleven-year-old son, Henry.

Edward de Vere died in his wife's house, King's Place, Hackney. He was buried in Hackney Church. It is said that his body was later removed to Westminster Abbey, but no record of this can be found.

His beautiful widow, still in her thirties, never married again. She seems to have been truly in love with her famous husband. And when she died, in 1612, it was found in her will that she wished "to be buried as near the body of my late dear and noble Lord and husband as may be."

An epitaph to Edward de Vere, Seventeenth Earl of Oxford, has been found in the Harleian Collection of Manuscripts:

> (Oxford) of whom I will only speak what all men's voices confirm, he was a man in mind and body absolutely accomplished with honourable endowments.

Henry Wriothesley, Third Earl of Southampton, in the Tower with his Cat.

From the painting in the collection of the Duke of Portland.

By courtesy of the owner, and the National Portrait Gallery.

The Earl of Oxford as Lord Great Chamberlain, Carrying the Sword of State before the Queen. 1578.

By courtesy of The British Museum.

Queen Elizabeth in Procession.

From the painting in the collection of Simon
Wingfield Digby, M.P.

*By courtesy of the owner. Photograph by Royal
Academy.*

Tis admired Emprese through the worlde applauded,
For supreme vertues, rarest Imitation
Whose Scepters rule fames loude-voyc'd trumpet laudeth
Vnto the eares of every forraigne Nation
Canopyed under powrfull Angells winges
To her Immortall praise sweete Science singes.

Willms   Rogers sculp

Queen Elizabeth in the late 1590's.

From the engraving by William Rogers.

By courtesy of the New York Public Library.

Chapter XVIII

THE SONNETS AND PLAYS

"Why write I still all one, ever the same,
And keep invention in a noted weed,
That every word doth almost tell my name,
Showing their birth, and where they did proceed?"

Sonnet 76.

If it be true that our hero, Edward de Vere, Seventeenth Earl of Oxford, *is* the author of the poems and plays that have come to be known to us as Shakespeare's, then how were they first presented to the public? This is a fair question, which we shall attempt to answer.

We have previously referred to the publication of *Venus and Adonis* and *Lucrece* during the period that negotiations were in progress to marry Oxford's daughter, Elizabeth de Vere, to the Earl of Southampton; hence, the dedication of each poem to that young nobleman. And remember that each of these appeared over the name of

William Shake-speare, a matter of significance that we have already discussed.

Now let us take the sonnets. It must have been known in London as early as 1598 that the Earl of Oxford had written those "sugar'd sonnets" mentioned by Francis Meres, and attributed by him to Shake-speare, with the suggestion that they were circulated among his private friends. It was, therefore, understood that they were composed for friendly eyes only, and probably contained references to persons and incidents well known in the early 1600's. Two of the sonnets did appear in print, in 1599, in *The Passionate Pilgrim*. They were numbers 138 and 144, and their text in this first printing differs in several lines from the same sonnets in the collection we know.

The first edition of the *collected* sonnets was a quarto that came out in 1609. The title page reads: [1] SHAKE-SPEARES/SONNETS/Neuer before Imprinted./At London/By G. Eld for T. T. and are/to be solde by John Wright, dwelling at Christ Church gate,/1609."
Overleaf we read: [2]

TO. THE. ONLIE. BEGETTER. OF. / THESE. INSUING. SONNETS./MR. W. H. ALL. HAPPINESSE. / AND. THAT. ETERNITIE. PROMISED. / BY. / OUR. EVER-LIVING. POET. / WISHETH. THE. WELL-WISHING. ADVEN-TURER. IN. / SETTING. FORTH. / T. T.

The questions begin. Who was "Mr. W. H.," the "onlie begetter"? Even before that, what is a "begetter"? After considerable research, the critics came to the conclusion that a begetter is just what it says he is, a getter.

---

1. The spelling and arrangement of lines is taken from the title-page of the original copy of the first quarto in the Elizabethan Club of Yale University.

2. Ibid.

In other words, Mr. W. H. *got* the poems for "T. T.," and for some years now, "T. T." has been identified as Thomas Thorpe, a stationer's assistant in London. So we return to "Mr. W. H." and whoever he might be. William Herbert, Earl of Pembroke? Henry Wriothesley, our old friend, Southampton, with his initials reversed? Both have been considered—and several others, too.

It was the eminent Shakespearean scholar, Sir Sidney Lee, who finally identified "Mr. W. H." as William Hall, an obscure printer and stationer, and friend of Thomas Thorpe. This identification becomes even clearer upon re-reading the dedication: "To . . . Mr. W. H. All Happinesse," or, running the letters together, Mr. W. Hall. It was many years before anything further was learned about Mr. Hall.

Not until the Oxford theory of authorship was presented and deemed worthy of study did anyone do any special research on Hackney where the famous earl had lived and died. Then it was found that a William Hall had indeed been a member of Hackney Church and had been married there in 1609. Further research produced the fascinating information that he had been not only a stationer and printer, but also a member of the government secret service.

The reader may recall that in 1605 there had been the historic Gunpowder Plot of *Don't you remember the fifth of November* fame. It had been a scheme of the Catholic faction, led by Guy Fawkes, to blow up Parliament, and certain well-known Catholics were on the wanted list for several years afterward, as conspirators.

We have said that the Earl of Oxford died in 1604 at King's Place, Hackney. We learn from records that his widow left Hackney in 1608, selling her estate there to Fulke Greville, Sir Philip Sidney's friend.

Now if Wliliam Hall living in Hackney saw that a

great mansion of the nobility was being evacuated, what was more natural to a secret service agent than to go in as the moving men were moving out and look around. Hall may even have had a suspicion that he might find evidence linked with the conspirators of the Gunpowder Plot. Opening a table drawer he found not the evidence he was looking for, but a collection of poems and three plays. The sonnets he took to his friend, Thomas Thorpe, to be printed and given to his bride as a wedding present later that year.

It is not our mission to follow through the steps which finally led to the publication of the sonnets in quarto in 1609. Certainly these poems must have been missed by the de Vere family, and realization of the extreme importance of anonymity was clear, due to the explicit allusions to incidents known and persons still living. Even posterity must not presume to guess at the secrets locked in these magic words; the fact of the author's relations with the late great Queen was damning enough to censor the whole collection. But published they were, and sold for five pence a copy, and the name of the author was the same as that given as the author of *Venus and Adonis* and *The Rape of Lucrece,* William Shake-speare. Moreover, the phrase, "ever-living poet" would seem to assume that the author is dead, living in eternity. The phrase could not describe the Stratford man because he was at that time very much alive. Many people in London both at Court and outside, must have realized that these sonnets reflect "a whole romance of personal experience," to use Saint-bury's words, and recognized only too well the circumstances and personages involved. A second edition was not attempted until 1640, by which time all the immediate relatives of Oxford had died. In the second edition the author's name is given as "Wil. Shake-speare, Gent." Note the hyphen each time, which differentiates this name from that of the Stratford man.

Exactly how the name became attached to the sonnets is a link in the mysterious chain that has not yet been discovered. It must have been known to "Mr. W. H." and to "T. T." that these poems were the work of the Earl of Oxford. A better educated man than they would have recognised that the sonnets were obviously by the same author as the two earlier poems, for which the author himself had chosen the nom de plume suggested by the Bolebec crest.

As noted before, Hall must have found not only the sonnets but three plays also, at Hackney. Twelve plays had already appeared in "memory-piracy" quartos, or at least, pirated editions unsanctioned by the author. And still more and more "stol'n and surreptitious" copies were slipping out into print one by one. Then there were those other plays left by the Earl of Oxford when he died, some not even ready to be published, which would need considerable editing. It was important to see that a correct edition of all the plays should be prepared and published.

It was fourteen years after the sonnet quarto came out that the first authentic edition of the Shakespeare plays was finally presented to the public in folio, in 1623. It is assumed that the four men responsible for organizing and publishing these plays were: William Stanley, Earl of Derby, Oxford's son-in-law, friend, and collaborator; Philip Herbert, Earl of Montgomery, another son-in-law; Philip's brother, William Herbert, Earl of Pembroke, another literary patron and author in Oxford's circle, who had for a little while been betrothed to Edward's daughter, Bridget; and Henry de Vere, the Eighteenth Earl of Oxford, Edward's son by Elizabeth Trentham.

153

To procure the most authentic copies of the plays, they appealed to the two foremost actor-managers in what had formerly been called the Chamberlain's Company: John Heminge and Henry Condell, both of whom had appeared many times at the Globe and Blackfriars with Burbage, Tarlton and Kempe. They were, therefore, thoroughly familiar with the dramas that had already been performed.

It must have been a terrific job to get the plays all together. Nineteen of the thirty-seven had already come out in quarto editions—good, bad and indifferent. When the Folio organizers came to write their address, *To The Great Variety of Readers,* they said:

> It had been a thing, we confess, worthy to have been wished that the author himself had lived to set forth and oversee his own writings. But since it hath been ordained otherwise, and he by death departed from that right, we pray you do not envy his friends the office or their care and pain to have collected and published them.

That statement certainly shows the trouble it had been to bring the plays together from their various sources, i.e., prompt books from the theatre's own library, transcripts of the author's manuscripts, printed quartos compared and corrected by memory of the parts as they were played, and from the author's own papers. The address goes on to say:

> His mind and hand went together, and what he thought he uttered with that easiness that we have scarce received from him a blot in his papers.

The promoters of the Folio couldn't have meant this literally because no author works that way, without making corrections. Moreover, Oxford probably employed professional copyists, who had learned to make a fair copy without a blot. They must have meant that the playwright wrote with ease and facility and that he did not make as many corrections as he might have done, had he not been summoned to attend the Queen, or to do all the hundreds of other things with which we know Edward de Vere involved himself.

Then there were the eighteen plays left by the author which had never before appeared in print. Some of these were finished masterpieces, like *King Lear*. Others were in various stages of composition, some perhaps scarcely started but with one or two exquisite passages which only he, the master, could have written. How these plays would have been pored over and polished by the eager friends and editors—some of the plays being brought up to date by allusions to recent happenings!

There should be a dedicatory poem addressed to the reader, which could be composed by a leading poet. Ben Jonson was chosen for that honor. Actually, Jonson and the great playwright had had little in common except genius. It is doubtful whether they ever met, though Jonson must have known that the author of the famous plays was the Earl of Oxford. Likewise, Edward would have known who Jonson was, or at least known of him as one of the younger playwrights. Jacques in *As You Like It* is purported to be a caricature of him, Jonson, whose ambition was to "cleanse the foul body of the infected world."

Jonson had been critical of Shakespeare, the author, heretofore, and would be again. Indeed, only a few years before the First Folio was published Jonson told the Scotsman, William Drummond of Hawthornden, that Shakespeare had no "art." By this Jonson meant, as he had said many times before, that Shakespeare did not observe "the unities." The European scholars, especially the Italians, had developed a whole set of dogmas on the subject of what was "correct" in composition of a drama. They decreed that the unities of time, place and action must be observed; that tragedy and comedy must never be mixed; and that certain limits must be set on characterization. These rigid rules shackled the genius of the European dramatists of this time.

But the poets and playwrights of England would be subject to arbitrary rules in literature no more than they were willing to abide by arbitrary laws of the land. Not even Jonson himself would be bound by all the classical restrictions. But both he and Sir Philip Sidney agreed with the Europeans who felt that all drama should have a moral purpose. As Sir Philip had written so gracefully:

Our poet . . . cometh to you with words set in delightful proportion. . . . With a tale, forsooth, he cometh unto you, with a tale which holdeth children from play and old men from the chimney-corner, and, pretending no more, doth intend the winning of the mind from wickedness to virtue.

But the great playwright could no more be bound by rules than could the mighty ocean itself. Nor could he bind himself to writing drama with a conventional moral tone, so long as his plays mirrored life and made its meaning clearer. He wrote to entertain, to stretch the imaginations of his audience . . . There were many arguments on these subjects over the years.

That was what Jonson had in mind when he told Drummond Shakespeare had no "art." Drummond was a great admirer of Shakespeare's genius; he owned copies of *Venus and Adonis, The Rape of Lucrece, Romeo and*

Juliet and *Love's Labour's Lost*. He was anxious to hear about the famous author from someone who might have known him in London, as he thought Jonson had. But all Jonson would say was to grumble about the playwright's carelessness in putting a seacoast in Bohemia "where there's no sea near by some hundred miles." He then told Drummond that was all he cared to say about Shakespeare. We have this conversation in detail because Drummond took notes of it.

But Jonson was perennially low in funds and had been subsidized by both the Herbert brothers and Henry de Vere. So he courteously accepted the commission and wrote a most glowing tribute to the playwright whom he had all but damned earlier. Jonson owed a good deal to the Herbert brothers; among other bounties, the Earl of Pembroke used to give him twenty pounds every Christmas to be spent just on books. During one of his prison terms Jonson had written to the Earl: "You have been ever free and noble to me."

However, Ben Jonson's tribute to the illustrious playwright is a masterpiece of innuendoes and double-entendres. He starts out by praising the playwright extravagantly:

> While I confess thy writing to be such
> As neither man nor muse can praise too much:
> Tis true, and all men's suffrage . . .
> Soul of the age!
> The applause, delight, the wonder of our stage!

He then compares the author to other members of Oxford's literary group:

> And tell how far thou didst our Lyly out-shine,
> Or sporting Kyd, or Marlowe's mighty line,

157

and places him beside the great classical authors, Aeschylus, Euripides and Sophocles. His statement, "And though thou hadst small Latin and less Greek," is disproved by the plays, a number of which, the scholars tell us, were taken from original classical sources.

Ben Jonson then proceeds to give his judgment of Shakespeare, which directly contradicts what he had said only a few years before:

> For a good poet's made, as well as born:
> And such wert thou. Look how the father's face
> Lives in his issue; even so the race
> Of Shakespeare's mind and manners brightly shines
> In his well-turned and true-filed lines.

The "Swan of Avon" allusion could refer, as we have learned, quite as aptly to Oxford as to the Stratford man. We recall that Oxford owned two estates on the Avon and another, Billesley Hall, four miles away from it. Let us repeat that Billesley Hall was noted in Elizabethan times for its extensive library, and that local tradition claims that *As You Like It* was written there.

However, a more plausible explanation of the "Swan of Avon" allusion is that Jonson had been told by the promoters to divert attention to the Stratford man as the author. We have discussed the reasons for this at some length in an earlier chapter.

The Earl of Oxford had previously been called the first in England who "knew Pindar's string," a poetic reference to the ancient Greek bard's harp. In addressing the playwright as "Swan," Jonson was boasting of his own knowledge that Horace, the adapter of Pindar, had described him (Pindar) as the Swan of Thebes "in a lovely ode in which he compared himself (Horace) to a small bee who makes lower sorties among the groves of flowers while the swan (Pindar) sings as he soars in effortless flights through the upper air to far places."

This is Jonson's passage:

> Sweet Swan of Avon! What a sight it were
> To see thee in our waters yet appear,
> And make those flights upon the banks of Thames
> That so did take Eliza and our James.

It was most appropriate that the First Folio of the great plays should be dedicated to the Herberts, "the incomparable pair of brethren." Both noble earls were patrons of literature. It was in their blood; they were nephews of Sir Philip Sidney and sons of his lovely sister, Mary Countess of Pembroke. The Earl of Pembroke especially, both before and after he became Lord Chamberlain, had done much to help struggling actors and playwrights.

Heminge and Condell did their best to preserve the plays they knew and loved. "His wit," they said of the famous playwright, "can no more lie hid than it could be lost." Yet without their help, many of these precious dramas might have lain "hid," completely lost to us today.

That First Folio of 1623 was a big undertaking. A. L. Rowse thinks that it must have been set by hand beginning several years before, surely as far back at 1619. Professor Benezet believes that it took four master printers and their apprentices at least two years to set up the type. Both agree that it had been an enormously expensive enterprise. It has been estimated that the cost came to between three and six thousand pounds. Copies were priced at twenty shillings each, but only six hundred were sold. Therefore, there must have been a staggering loss to somebody. It was not the printer who lost money on the project; he bought a fine house shortly after publication, indicating that he made money on it. It couldn't have been the Shakespeare family of Stratford, none of whom, so far as we know, ever even saw a copy of the First Folio. It was not Ben Jonson, who never would have had enough money to finance the cost in the first place, and we have every reason to believe that he was well paid for the commission of writing the dedicatory poem.

Then it must have been three of the four noble earls who put up the money for publication. The Earls of Derby, Montgomery and Pembroke were said to be the three most affluent noblemen in England at that time. The loss of two thousand pounds apiece would have been no more than any of them could afford.

Moreover, they had the inestimable satisfaction of knowing that the finest dramas in the English language—perhaps in any language—would be preserved for generations yet unborn, thanks to them.

It is the critical Ben Jonson who gives the final epitaph:

He was not of an age, but for all time.[3]

---

3. From the Preface to the First Folio.

Chapter XIX

THE PORTRAITS

"Look here, upon this picture, and on this,
The counterfeit presentment . . .
See what a grace was seated on this brow."
Hamlet.

As we promised, we have attempted to bring to you the story of Edward de Vere, the Seventeenth Earl of Oxford, begging you to fill in with your own imagination the yawning gaps in the biography. We have affirmed our belief that this noble peer is the true author of the plays and poems we know as Shakespeare's. Yet we emphasize that we are presenting to you a *story* and not a brief to prove an argument.

Notwithstanding, the biography of Edward de Vere would be incomplete without considering the evidence of the portraits.

Of all the many portraits of William Shakespeare, only

two have any claim to authenticity: i.e., the Droeshout engraving in the First Folio, and the bust above his grave in Holy Trinity, Stratford. These two representations bear not the slightest resemblance to each other. The only features common to them are the bald head and unusually high forehead befitting to a man of great brains.

The Stratford bust has been proved to be a copy of the original monument. The first bust was of alabaster according to a number of contemporary records, the present bust of a different kind of stone. There are a number of other discrepancies which can be noted by comparing the present bust with the engravings of the original in Sir William Dugdale's *Antiquities of Warwickshire,* published in 1635. The moustache turns up instead of down; the hair has been curled above the ears; the snub nose, pouches under the eyes, fat cheeks and chin contrast with the hard face of the original, while its air of complacency caused the Shakespearean scholar, J. Dover Wilson, to refer to it as a "self-satisfied pork butcher."

The engraving in the First Folio is the work of Droeshout, a Dutchman who was only fifteen years old when Shakespeare died. Whether he ever visited Stratford or London, or whether he was given a preliminary sketch for the engraving he was to do seven years later, we do not know. In this engraving he gives Shakespeare a hair style of the Netherlands, quite unknown in England. While the ruff is that of an English nobleman, it is drawn so that we have the impression of a severed head floating in air.

Ben Jonson wrote of this engraving:

> This Figure, that thou here seest put,
> It was for gentle Shakespeare cut;
> Wherein the Graver had a strife
> With Nature, to out-do the life;

> O, could he but have drawn his wit
>   As well in brass, as he hath hit
> His face, the Print would then surpass
>   All that was ever writ in brasse.
> But since he cannot, Reader, looke
>   Not on his Picture, but his Booke.

Note that Jonson does not say: "This is a portrait of Shakespeare," or even "a likeness." But "this Figure . . . was . . . cut for" him, i.e., in place of him. And indeed, the Graver seems to have had quite a struggle with Nature. For let us look more closely. What is that strong line from the tip of the left ear to the chin? Was there ever such a line in human anatomy? Does it not suggest a mask? No wonder Jonson asks the Reader to "looke, not on his Picture, but his Booke." [1]

But these arguments are negative. And actually there is positive evidence.

It is to our own countryman, Charles Wisner Barrell, Secretary-Treasurer of the Shakespeare Fellowship, that we owe the modern and scientific research which proves this positive evidence. Remembering the patrician features, auburn hair and hazel eyes common to most of the portraits of Shakespeare, and remembering their marked resemblance to the portraits of the Earl of Oxford, Mr. Barrell, after months of negotiation, finally obtained permission to X-ray three of these Shakespeare portraits. The result of his infra-red and X-ray plates must be given in detail. [2]

After studying all the Shakespeare portraits, Mr. Bar-

---

1. *Shake-speare, the Man Behind the Name,* by Dorothy Ogburn and Charlton Ogburn, Jr.

2. For the story of Charles Wisner Barrell's X-ray and infra-red photographs, see *Scientific American,* January, 1940.

rell chose three which he felt might reveal overpainting under the penetrating X-rays. These portraits were the Hampton Court, owned by the Royal Family, and the Janssen and Ashbourne portraits, owned by the Folger Shakespeare Library in Washington, D. C. Expert examination proved that all three had been altered by the same "furtive hand."

The Hampton Court Portrait.

This portrait shows the Bard dressed as a nobleman, holding two swords. He has a bald head, short nose and bourgeois collar. One of the swords is a gentleman's fighting rapier; the other has a coal black blade, sharp point, and a long hilt with a ball on the top.

The X-rays reveal that the head was originally covered with auburn hair, the nose longer by a good fraction of an inch, closely resembling the Ashbourne portrait. The hazel eyes, auburn-colored beard and ruddy cheeks resemble the known portraits of the Earl of Oxford.

Underneath the painted sloping collar is a nobleman's fluted ruff. But most interesting of all is the revelation that the sword in the right hand is actually the Sword of State painted over with lampblack. This Sword we know well from other contemporary pictures. It was carried only by the Lord Great Chamberlain of the Realm, the Seventeenth Earl of Oxford during most of the reign of Queen Elizabeth, who, by his office and by his seniority, took precedence over all other earls. Of the seven known portraits of Oxford, three show the Sword in his right hand, as it is in this Hampton Court portrait known as Shakespeare's.

Is it likely that a man from the country with no pretensions to aristocracy would be allowed to have his portrait painted dressed as a nobleman and carrying the recognised Sword of State? He would have been clapped into jail if ever he had appeared dressed this way in London.

The Janssen Portrait.

This picture represents a handsome man of about forty, wearing a collar of delicate lace. The head is bald; the only hair showing, auburn; the beard, light brown; eyes, hazel, cheeks, pink. Above and to the left of the head in upright characters we read: "A E 46," and below in slanting figures, the date, "1610." As far back as the year 1909 (as described in *The Connoisseur* of that year) and long before X-rays were being used on paintings, it was discovered that the inscription "46" had been tampered with, the original figure being written "A E 40."

What the X-ray revealed here was that the original inscription was indeed "A E 40," but the date "1590." At that time Oxford would have been forty years old. The tampering with the date is confirmed by another anachronism. The lace of the collar contains the Tudor rose, the emblem worn by courtiers to Queen Elizabeth. Had the portrait been painted as the false date indicated, i.e., in 1610, instead of the rose in the lace collar, there would have been the Scottish thistle, emblem of King James I. Needless to add, the bald head under X-rays showed a full crop of auburn hair beneath.

The Ashbourne Portrait.

This painting under X-rays reveals even more interesting facts than the other two. As it stands, the Ashbourne portrait shows an aristocrat in dress and appearance, with bald head and high forehead. The gauntlets of a noble-man dangle from his hands, a nobleman's ring is on his thumb, a nobelman's rapier belt around his waist. In contrast, there is a ruff of the style worn by small tradesmen in the year 1611, the date of the portrait as it stands. In that year the Stratford man would have been forty-seven, about the right age for the aristocrat in the portrait.

But this is what the infra-red plate shows:

1. A wide courtier's ruff under the flimsy bourgeois ruff, of the style that a courtier to Queen Elizabeth would have worn, but not worn in the reign of King James.
2. A head of thick auburn hair under the bald head.
3. The eye, ears, snout and tusk of a boar's head under the blurred face on the seal ring.
4. Under the date, "1611," a hole in the canvas, showing that an earlier date had been erased with vigor before the later date was painted in.
5. Below the date, a coat of arms surmounted by a griffin's head, supported on one side by a large cat-like beast; on the other, by a griffin. On the shield are three beaked heads, torn off instead of being cut straight across, two side by side, the third below, all facing left.
6. Below the coat of arms there is a monogram, which is probably the painter's signature. The letters are "C" and "K" overlapping a little, with the "C" slightly to the left and above the "K."
7. The gold of the book cover held by the nobleman, and the gold of the ring on his thumb, was originally a true lemon gold, instead of the orange gold we see today.

The discovery of the nobleman's ruff of an earlier time than the faked date of the painting, "1611," together with the thumb ring which could have been worn *only* by an

166

English nobleman of high degree, proves that the portrait could not have been a likeness of the Warwickshire man.

It was noted by the experts that the *revealed* nobleman's ruff around the neck, matches the still present ruffs around the wrists, being the same style and material.

The signet ring is particularly interesting because, as we have noted, it could have been worn only by "an exalted personage." Therefore, Mr. Barrell was not surprised to find underneath the paint on the seal, the head of a wild boar, one of the crests of the de Veres.

The coat of arms was not immediately identified, but the College of Heralds found that the crest might have been that of either of two Staffordshire families, i.e., the Sneyds of Keel Hall, or the Trenthams of Rocester Abbey. Then it was discovered that Elizabeth Trentham, Oxford's second wife, was a member of both the Sneyd and the Trentham families, so that the arms of both families belonged to her through both lines of descent.

Mr. Barrell found out further in a book called *The Bearing of Coat Armour by Ladies* that originally there was no provision for women to bear arms. But "if the lady were an heiress, or owned lands, her husband bore her arms for her." An example of this usage is the fact that Richard Neville, the "King Maker," carried the Beauchamp arms of his wife and the Montague arms of his mother on his great seal instead of his own coat of arms.

The signature of the artist, "C K" was recognized as the monogram of Cornelius Ketel, one of Holland's most famous portrait painters. In the *Nouvelle Biographie Generale* we read of Ketel:

La reine Elizabeth, le comte d'Oxford, les principaux seigneurs et dames de la cour lui firent executer leurs portraits.

167

Shakespeare isn't even mentioned as having been a subject painted by Ketel, while the noble Earl of Oxford is.

Further proof of the portrait being an original by Ketel is contained in a book by Karel Van Mander, a talented Dutch painter, called *Lives of the Most Celebrated Modern Painters,* published in 1604. Van Mander writes:

> Ketel also made a portrait of the Duke of Oxford (Edward de Vere), the High Chancellor (Sir Christopher Hatton), and of many other important members of the nobility. Some of these portraits were life sized and full length.

We know Ketel's portrait of Sir Christopher Hatton, and it resembles the Ashbourne portrait of Shakespeare in many respects. Still further examination of the Ashbourne reveals that it has been cut off, suggesting that it might have been one of the "life sized and full length" portraits Van Mander refers to. Perhaps there may have been some detail in the lower part of the portrait which could have betrayed the original subject. Hatton's portrait bears his name on a light-colored background; possibly the Ashbourne showed a similar inscription bearing Oxford's name. Doubtless it was easier to cut off than to paint over the telltale feature.

Mr. Barrell then placed the Ashbourne portrait between copies of two of the known portraits of Oxford. Where there were differences they occurred between the two Oxford portraits and not btween the Ashbourne and either one of the Oxford portraits. The only real differences were the high forehead and bald head, and these, as explained above, are proved by the X-rays to have been part of the deception.

168

We have now considered three of the many existing portraits known as representations of the famous author and playwright. We assert of these three that instead of being likenesses of William Shakespeare, it is highly probable that they are actually portraits of Edward de Vere, Seventeenth Earl of Oxford, Lord Great Chamberlain, and Courtier to the Queen.

Introduction to Cardanus' Comfort.

This is the introduction that Oxford wrote for the translation of Thomas Bedingfield's *Cardanus' Comfort*. Oxford was only twenty-two when he wrote it and the poem accompanying it, the latter given in the text of this biography:

> To my loving friend Thomas Bedingfield Esquire, one of Her Majesty's Pensioners.
> After I had perused your letters, good Master Bedingfield, finding in them your request for differing from the desert of your labour, I could not choose but greatly doubt whether it were better for me to yield to your desire, or execute mine own intention toward the publishing of your book . . . And when you examine yourself—what doth avail a mass of gold to be continually imprisoned in your bags and never to be employed to your use? Wherefore we have this Latin proverb: *scire tuum nihil est, nisi te scire hoc sciat alter.*

What doth avail the tree unless it yield fruit unto another? What doth avail the vine unless another delighteth in the grape? What doth avail the rose unless another took pleasure in the smell? Why should this tree be accounted better than that tree but for goodness of his fruit? Why should this rose be better esteemed than that rose, unless in pleasantness of smell it far surpassed the other rose? And so it is in all things as well as in Man. Why should this man be more esteemed than that man, but for his virtue through which every man desireth to be accounted of? Then you amongst men, I do not doubt, but will aspire to follow that virtuous path, to illuster yourself with the ornaments of virtue. And in mine opinion as it beautieth a fair woman to be decked with pearls and precious stones, so much more it ornifieth a gentleman to be furnished with glittering virtues.

Wherefore, considering the small harm I do to you, the great good I do to others, I prefer mine own intention to discover your volume, before your request to secret same.

This quotation is taken from *Lord Oxford and the Shakespeare Group,* by Lieut.-Colonel Montagu W. Douglas, G S I, C I E., Third Edition, The Alden Press (Oxford), Ltd., 1952.

Note how frequently Oxford refers to the rose and its cultivation. Oxford would have been well-versed in rose culture, having been brought up in Cecil House, whose rose garden was tended by the famous gardener, Gerard.

We here present a few of the shorter poems of the young Earl of Oxford, and also poetry composed by friends and contemporaries of his mentioned in the biography. The verses are chosen, not for their literary excellence, but because each poem seems to express the character of its writer, or to refer to an incident described in the text.

Fancy and Desire.

Come hither, shepherd's swayne:
   "Sir, what do you require?"
I pray thee, shew to me thy name.
   "My name is Fond Desire."

When wert thou borne, Desire?
   "In pompe and pride of May."
By whom, sweet boy, wert thou begot?
   "By fond Conceit men say."

Tell me who was thy nurse?
   "Fresh youth in sugar'd joy."
What was thy meate and dayly foode?
   "Sad sighs with great annoy."

What hadst thou then to drinke?
   "Unsavoury lovers teares."
What cradle wert thou rocked in?
   "In hope devoyde of feares."

What lulld thee then asleepe?
   "Sweet speech, which likes me best."
Tell me, where is thy dwelling place?
   "In gentle hartes I rest."

What thing doth please thee most?
   "To gaze on beauty stille."
Whom dost thou thinke to be thy foe?
   "Disdain of my good wille."

Doth company displease?
   "Yes, surelye, many one."
Where doth Desire delight to live?
   "He loves to live alone."

Doth either tyme or age
   Bring him unto decaye?
"No, no Desire both lives and dyes
   Ten thousand times a daye."

Then, fond Desire, farewelle,
   Thou are no mate for mee;
I sholde be lothe, methinkes,, to dwelle
   With such a one as thee.

This poem is taken from *Reliques of Ancient English Poetry*, Series the Second, Book I. With this notation: "Edward Earl of Oxford, was in high fame for his poetical talents in the reign of Elizabeth: . . . To gratify curiousity, we have inserted a sonnet of his, which is quoted with great encomiums for its 'excellencie and wit,' in Puttenham's *Arte of Engl. Poesie* (Lond. 1589) and found entire in the *Garland of Good-Will*. A few more of his sonnets (distinguished by the initials E.O.) may be seen in the *Paradise of Daintie Devises*."

Megliora Spero.

Faction that ever dwells in Court where wit excels,
    Hath set defiance.
Fortune and Love have sworn that they were never born
    Of one alliance.

Cupid which doth aspire to be god of Desire,
    Swears he "gives laws:
That were his arrows hit, some joy, some sorrow it:
    Fortune no cause."

Fortune swears "weakest heart," the books of Cupid's arts
    Turned with her wheel,
Senseless themselves shall prove, Venture hath place in
      love.
    Ask them that feel!"

This discord it begot atheists, that honour not.
    Nature thought good
Fortune should ever dwell in Court where wits excel:
    Love keep the wood.

So to the wood went I, with Love to live and die,
    Fortune's forlorn.
Experience of my youth made me think humble Truth
    In deserts born.

My saint I keep to me, and Joan herself is free,
    Joan fair and true!
She that doth only move passions of love with Love.
    Fortune, adieu!

FINIS

E. O.

From *Some Shorter Elizabethan Poems*, ed. A. H. Bullen.

The following poem was published in *The Phoenix Nest*, 1593.

What cunning can express
    The favour of her face?
To whom, in this distress,
    I do appeal for grace.
        A thousand Cupids fly
        About her gentle eye.

From whence, each throws a dart
    That kindleth soft sweet fire
Within my sighing heart
    Possessed by desire.
        No sweeter life I try
        Than in her love to die.

The lily in the field
    That glories in his white;
For pureness now must yield
    And render up his right.
        Heaven pictured in her face
        Doth promise joy and grace.

Fair Cynthia's silver light
    That beats on running streams,
Compares not with her white,
    Whose hairs are all sunbeams.
        Her virtues so do shine
        As day unto mine eyne.

With this there's a red
 Exceeds the damask rose:
Which in her cheeks is spread,
 Whence every favour grows.
  In sky there is no star
  That she surmounts not far.

When Phoebus from the bed
 Of Thetis doth arise;
The morning blushing red
 In fair carnation-wise,
  He shows it in her face
  As queen of every grace.

This pleasant lily white
 This taint of roseate red,
This Cynthia's silver light
 The sweet fair Dea spread,
  These sunbeams in mine eye;
  These beauties make me die.

E. O.

From *Some Shorter Elizabethan Poems,* ed. A. H. Bullen.

Love and Antagonism.

The trickling tears that fall along my cheeks,
    The secret sighs that show my inward grief,
The present pains perforce that Love aye seeks,
    Bid me renew my cares without relief;
In woeful song, in dole display,
My pensive heart for to betray.

Betray thy grief, thy woeful heart with speed;
    Resign thy voice to her that caused thee woe;
With irksome cries, bewail thy late done deed,
    For she thou lov'st is sure thy mortal foe;
And help for thee there is none sure,
But still in pain thou must endure.

The stricken deer hath help to heal his wound,
    The haggard hawk with toil is made full tame;
The strongest tower, the cannon lays on ground,
    The wisest wit that ever had the fame,
Was thrall to Love by Cupid's slights;
Then weigh my cause with equal weights.

She is my joy, she is my care and woe;
    She is my pain, she is my ease therefore;
She is my death, she is my life also,
    She is my salve, she is my wounded sore;
In fine, she hath the hand and knife
That may both save and end my life.

And shall I live on earth to be her thrall?
　　And shall I live and serve her all in vain?
And shall I kiss the steps that she lets fall,
　　And shall I pray the Gods to keep the pain
From her, that is so cruel still?
No, no, on her work all your will.

And let her feel the power of all your might,
　　And let her have her most desire with speed
And let her pine away both day and night,
　　And let her moan, and none lament her need;
And let all those that shall her see,
Despise her state and pity me.

                                                                E. O.

From *Shake-speare, The Man Behind The Name,* by Dorothy and
Charlton Ogburn, Jr.
Note st. 5, line 1. "Shall I live . . . to be her thrall?" Again the
play on Anne Vavasor's name, which meant "master of vassals."
The Ogburns find comparable lines from *Twelfth Night, Much Ado,
Taming of the Shrew, Two Gentlemen of Verona,* and *Lucrece.*

Revenge of Wrong

Fain would I sing, but fury makes me fret,
   And rage hath sworn to seek revenge of wrong;
My mazèd mind in malice is so set,
   As Death shall daunt my deadly dolours long;
Patience perforce is such a pinching pain,
As die I will, or suffer wrong again.

I am no sot, to suffer such abuse
   As doth bereave my heart of his delight;
Nor will I frame myself to such as use,
   With calm consent, to suffer such despite;
No quiet sleep shall once possess mine eye
Till Wit hath wrought his will on injury.

My heart shall fail, and hand shall lose his force,
   But some device shall pay Despite his due;
And Fury shall consume my careful corse,
   Or raze the ground whereon my sorrow grew.
Lo, thus in rage of ruthful mind refus'd,
I rest reveng'd on whom I am abus'd.

                                        Earle of Oxenforde.

From *Shake-speare, The Man Behind the Name.*
The Ogburns' careful research notes comparisons with:
Hamlet (IV, 4.65-66):

               O! from this time forth,
      My thoughts be bloody, or be nothing worth!

and *Hamlet* (III.1.124-25):
   I am very proud, revengeful, ambitious.

and Sonnet 147.

   Past cure I am, now that reason is past care,
   And frantic mad with evermore unrest . . .

Verses Made By The Earl of Oxforde.

Sitting alone upon my thought in melancholy mood,
In sight of sea, and at my back an ancient hoary wood,
I saw a fair young lady come, her secret fears to wail,
Clad all in colour of a nun, and covered with a veil;
Yet (for the day was calm and clear) I might discern her
    face,
As one might see a damask rose hid under crystal glass.

Three times, with her soft hand, full hard on her left
    side she knocks,
And sigh'd so sore as might have mov'd some pity in the
    rocks:
From sighs and shedding amber tears into sweet song
    she brake,
When thus the echo answered her to every word she spake:

ANNE VAVASOR'S ECHO

O heavens! who was the first that bred in me this fever?
    Vere.
Who was the first that gave the wound whose fear I wear
    for ever? Vere.
What tyrant, Cupid, to my harm usurps thy golden quiver?
    Vere.
What wight first caught this heart and can from bondage
    it deliver? Vere.

Yet who doth most adore this wight, oh hollow caves tell
  true? You.
What nymph deserves his liking best, yet doth in sorrow
  rue? You.
What makes him not regard good will with some regard
  of ruth? Youth.
What makes him show besides his birth, such pride and
  such untruth? Youth.

May I his favour match with love, if he my love will try?
  Ay.
May I requite his birth with faith? Then faithful will I
  die? Ay.

  And I that knew this lady well,
  Said, Lord, how great a miracle,
  To hear how Echo told the truth,
  As true as Phoebus' oracle.

This poem again taken from the Ogburns' *Shake-speare, The Man
Behind The Name,* who note that it is taken from the *Rawlinson
MS.* They further note that *Vere* is pronounced *Vair.* This we have
heard disputed, by an authority on Elizabethan English, who believes that at Court this pronunciation would have been *Vere,* as
in *here.*

The Ogburns, however, have found comparisons of this poem
with *Venus and Adonis,* st. 139, 140, 142.

139 And now she beats her heart, whereat it groans,
    That all the neighbour caves, as seeming troubled,
    Make verbal repetition of her moans:
    Passion on passion deeply is redoubled:
      "Ay me!" she cries, and twenty times, "Woe, woe!"
      And twenty echoes twenty times cry so.

140 . . . Her heavy anthem still concludes in woe,
    And still the choir echoes answer so.

142 She says, " 'Tis so:" they answer all, " 'Tis so;"
    And would say after her, if she said "No."

By Anne Vavasor

Tho' I seem strange, sweet friend, be thou not so,
Do not accoy thyself with sullen will;
Mine harte hath vowed, although my tongue says noe,
To be thine own in friendly liking still.

Thou seest me live amongst the lynxes' eyes
That pry into the privy thoughts of mynde;
Thou knowst right well what sorrows may arise
If once they chance my settled looks to find.

Content thyself that once I made an oath
To shield myself in shroud of honest shame,
And when thou list make trial of my troth
So that thou save the honour of my name.

And let me sense although I be not coy
To cloak my sad conceits with smiling cheer;
Let not my gestures show wherein I joy,
Nor by my looks let not my love appear.

We silly dames that fall suspect do fear
And live within the might of envy's lake,
Must in our hartes a secret meaning bear
Far from the rest which outwardly we make.

So were I like, I list not vaunt my love
Where I desire there most I feign debate,
One hath my hand, another hath my glove,
But by my harte whom I seem most to hate.

Thus, farewell, friend! I will continue strange;
Thou shalt not hear my words or writing ought;
Let it suffice my vow shall never change;
As for the rest I leave it to thy thought.

From *The Spenser Anthology*, ed. by Edward Alber.

By William Cecil, Lord Burghley

To Mistress Anne Cecil, upon Making her a New Year's Gift.
Written in 1568; Lansdowne MS. 104.

As years do grow, so cares increase;
   And time will move to look to thrift:
Though years in me work nothing less,
   Yet, for your years, and New Year's gift,
   This house wife's toy is now my chift!
      To set you on work, some thrift to feel,
      I send you now a spinning wheel.

But one thing first, I wish and pray,
   Lest thirst of thrift might soon you tire,
Only to spin one pound a day,
   And play the rest, as time require:
   Sweat not! (oh fie!) fling rocks in fire!
      God send, who send'th all thrift and wealth,
      You, long years; and your father, health!

---

1. In 1571 Mistress Anne Cecil married Edward de Vere, Seventeenth Earl of Oxford.

This poem is from *The Oxford Book of Sixteenth Century Verse,* chosen by E. K. Chambers.

By John Lyly

From *Campaspe,* 1584.

Granichus O! for a bowl of fat Canary,
Rich Palermo, sparkling Sherry,
Some nectar else, from Juno's dairy.
O! these draughts would make us merry

Psyllus O! for a wench (Ideal in faces,
And in other daintier things);
Tickled am I with her embraces
Fine dancing in such fairy rings.

Manes O! for a plump fat leg of mutton,
Veal, lamb, capon, pig or coney;
None is happy but a glutton,
None an ass but who wants money.

Chorus Wines (indeed) and girls are good,
But brave victuals feast the blood;
For wenches, wine and lusty cheer,
Jove would leap down to surfeit here.

From *The Oxford Book of Sixteenth Century Verse.*

By Anthony Munday

E xcept I should in friendship seem ingrate,
D enying duty, whereto I am bound;
W ith letting slip your Honour's worthy state,
A t all assays, which I have noble found,
R ight well I might refrain to handle pen:
D enouncing aye the company of men.

D own, dire despair, let courage come in place,
E xalt his fame whom Honour doth embrace.

V irtue hath aye adorn'd your valiant heart,
E xampl'd by your deed of lasting fame:
R egarding such as take God Mars his part
E ach where by proof, in honour and in name.

This poem appeared in the 1590's, in *The Mirror of Mutability*. I have taken it from *This Star of England*, by kind permission of the authors, Dorothy and Charlton Ogburn.

LOVE THY CHOICE

Who taught thee first to sigh, alas, my heart?
    Who taught thy tongue the woeful words of plaint?
Who filled your eyes with tears of bitter smart?
    Who gave thee grief and made thy joys to faint?
Who first did paint with colours pale thy face?
    Who first did break thy sleeps of quiet rest?
Above the rest in court who gave thee grace?
    Who made thee strive in honour to be best?
In constant truth to bide so firm and sure,
    To scorn the world regarding but thy friends?
With patient mind each passion to endure,
    In one desire to settle to the end?
Love then thy choice wherein such choice thou bind,
    As nought but death shall ever change thy mind.

Earle of Oxenforde.

From *Shake-speare, The Man Behind the Name.*

The Ogburns append this note: "Sonnet in the Shakespearean form. It could well have been addressed to the Queen, who was said to have 'wooed the Earl of Oxford' when he was a young courtier."

Note line 9 "in constant truth," and also the last four lines, which seem to express Oxford's philosophy even at this early age.

WOMAN'S CHANGEABLENESS

If women could be fair and yet not fond,
    Or that their love were firm and fickle, still,
I would not marvel that they make men bond,
    By service long to purchase their good will;
But when I see how frail those creatures are,
I muse that men forget themselves so far.

To make the choice they make, and how they change,
    How oft from Phoebus do they flee to Pan,
Unsettled still like haggards wild they range,
    These gentle birds that fly from man to man;
Who would not scorn and shake them from the fist
And let them fly fair fools which way they list.

Yet for disport we fawn and flatter both,
    To pass the time when nothing else can please,
And train them to our lure with subtle oath,
    Till, weary of their wiles, ourselves we ease;
And then we say when we their fancy try,
To play with fools, O what a fool was I.

Earle of Oxenforde.

This was the poem which convinced J. T. Looney that the Earl
of Oxford had written Shakespeare's plays.
Compare Sonnet 137.

BIBLIOGRAPHY

Irwin Anthony: *Raleigh and His World.*
John Aubrey: *Brief Lives,* ed. by Andrew Clark. 2 vols. 1898.
Sir Francis Bacon: *Essayes,* 1597-1625, ed. J. M. Dent, London 1897.
Granville Barker and G. B. Harrison: *A Companion to Shakespeare Studies.*
Louis P. Benezet: *The Six Loves of "Shake-speare."* 1958.
Ivor Brown: *Shakespeare, a Biography and an Interpretation.* 1949.
A. H. Bullen: Ed. *Some Shorter Elizabethan Poems.*
M. St. Clare Byrne: *Elizabethan Life in Town and Country.* 1950.
Sir Edmund K. Chambers: *Biography of Sir Henry Lee.* 1936.
————: *The Elizabethan Stage.* 3 vols.
————: Ed. *The Oxford Book of Sixteenth Century Verse.*
————: *Shakespeare Gleanings.* 1944.
Rev. William Henry Charlton: *Burghley.* Stamford, England. 1847.
G. H. Chettle: *Hampton Court Palace.*
Marchette Chute: *Ben Jonson of Westminster.* 1953.

————: *Shakespeare of London*. 1949.

Mandell Creighton: *Queen Elizabeth*. 1920.

Emma Marshall Denkinger: *Immortal Sidney*. 1931.

Montagu W. Douglas: *Lord Oxford and the Shakespeare Group*. 1952.

Edward Dowden: *Shakespeare*.

Sir Edwin Durning-Lawrence, Bt.: *The Shakespeare Myth*.

Eight Famous Elizabethan Plays. Introduction by Esther Cloudman Dunn. Modern Library, N. Y. 1932.

A. J. Evans: *Shakespeare's Magic Circle*. 1956.

Edmund H. Fellowes: *The English Madrigal*. 1935.

H. N. Gibson: *The Shakespeare Claimants*. 1962.

J. R. Green: *Short History of the English People*. N. Y. 1884.

F. E. Halliday: *Shakespeare, a pictorial biography*. 400th Anniversary edition. 1964.

The History and Treasures of Hatfield House.

Hiram Haydn: Ed. *The Portable Elizabethan Reader*. 1946.

J. Leslie Hotson: *The First Night of Twelfth Night*. 1961.

William Kent and others: *Edward de Vere, Seventeenth Earl of Oxford, The Real Shakespeare*. 1957.

Sir Sidney Lee: Ed. *Elizabethan Sonnets*.

————: *A Life of Shakespeare*. 1908.

Sir John Neale: *The London of Elizabeth I*. 1959.

————: *Queen Elizabeth*. 1934.

Allardyce Nicoll: *Shakespeare*. 1952.

Dorothy and Charlton Ogburn: *This Star of England*. 1950.

Dorothy and Charlton Ogburn, Jr.: *Shake-speare, The Man Behind the Name*. 1962.

James M. Purcell: *Sidney's Stella*. 1934.

Peter Quennell: *Shakespeare, a Biography*. 1963.

Reliques of Ancient English Poetry. The Sixth Edition. 4 vols. London, 1823.

A. L. Rowse: *The England of Elizabeth*. 1950.

————: *William Shakespeare*. 1963.

Sir Arthur Quiller-Couch: Ed. *The Oxford Book of English Verse*.

Shakespeare's England. by various authors. 2 vols. Oxford, Clarendon Press.

Sir Philip Sidney: *Arcadia*. 1593. Ed. by Albert Feuillerat, N. Y. 1922.

Edith Sitwell: *The Queens and the Hive*. 1962.

Sir Edmund Spenser: *The Faerie Queene*. Cambridge ed.

The Spenser Anthology, Ed. by Edward Alber, London, 1901.

Lytton Strachey: *Elizabeth and Essex, a Tragic History.*

Mary Sturt: *Francis Bacon.* 1932.

The Tower of London. Ministry of Works Guide-Book. 1962.

Milton Waldman: *Elizabeth and Leicester.* 1945.

————: *England's Elizabeth.* 1933.

Mrs. A. Murray Smith and Lady Birchenough: *The Westminster Abbey Guide.* 34th edition. 1959.

John Dover Wilson: *The Essential Shakespeare.*

Violet A. Wilson: *Society Women of Shakespeare's Time.* 1925.

Texts from the Plays are taken from *The Yale Shakespeare,* ed. by members of the English Faculty, Yale University.

Special material is taken from the *Sonnets,* in this same edition, edited by Edward Bliss Reed.

The Shakespeare Appendix. Various authors.

Shakespeare Cross-Examination: A compilation of articles first appearing in the *American Bar Association Journal.* Cuneo Press, Inc. Chicago 1961.

Special articles on Edward de Vere and Henry Wriothesley and Robert Devereux in the *Encyclopaedia Britannica,* 9th and 11th editions.

Articles from the *Dictionary of National Biography.*

Special references from Burke's *Peerage.*

Roy Strong: *The Portraits of Queen Elizabeth I,* 1963.

Bacon, Sir Francis, advice on Essex, 134; prosecution at trial of Essex, 138.

Bacon, Sir Nicholas, 23.

Bedingfield, Thomas, 39-41; 169-170.

Bolebec, Viscount, 8; 94; pun on crest of, 38; 143.

Burghley, See Cecil, Sir William.

Cambridge, University of, customs, 19-22.

Catholicism, 90; Gunpowder Plot, 151.

Cecil, Anne, at Cecil House, 15; marriage negotiations, 36; marriage, 37; request for lodgings, Hampton Court, 40-41; humiliation of, 45, 47; Oxford's return to, 59-60; death, 69.

Cecil, Lady Mildred, 69; 112.

Cecil, Sir Robert, 15; accused by Essex, 137; teased by Queen, 142; in Queen's last illness, 146.

Cecil, Sir Wiliam, First Baron Burghley, at Hedingham, 9; London house, 12-16; Harvey's pun on *Polus*, 39; announces Anne's pregnancy, 42; scorned by son-in-law, 45; chides Oxford, 64; refers to "lewd companions," 65; death of wife and daughter, 69; tribute to son-in-law, 120; life of, 109-120; resignation, 110; birth and early career, 110; at Cambridge, 110; first marriage, 112; relations with Princess Elizabeth, 113; Principle Secretary to Queen, 9; Lord Treasurer, 115; entertains Queen, 15; characteristics, 115; letter to Walsingham, 115; relations with Oxford, 118; death, 119; poem to Anne, 185.

Chapman, George, description of Oxford in *Bussy d'Amboise*, 44; member of Oxford group, 65.

Churchyard, Thomas, 66.

Clark, Bartholomew, 38-40.

Derby, William Stanley, Earl of, member of Oxford group, 2; 67; marriage to Elizabeth de Vere, 98; friendship with Oxford, 105; responsibility for First Folio, 105; 153; 160.

de Vere, Lady Bridget, 105.

de Vere, Sir Edward, birth, 56; devotion of Oxford to, 81-82; in Woodstock, 83-84; at University of Leyden, 85; joins army, 87; decorated for gallantry, 80; knighted, 88; death, 88.

de Vere, Lady Elizabeth, betrothed to Southampton, 91; betrothal broken, 97; marries Lord Derby, 98-99; incident at Court, 143.

de Vere, Lady Susan, marries Earl of Montgomery, 105.

Drummond, William, 155-157.

Dudley, Robert, Earl of Leicester, at Hedingham 9; host to Queen, 26; introduces step-son, 129; Commander in Chief, Netherlands, 90.

Elizabeth Tudor, see Queen Elizabeth.

Essex, Robert Devereux, Earl of, 129-130; friendship with Southampton, 92; March on City, 136-139; trial of, 136-137.

Farmer, John, composer, 69.

First Folio, 153-160.

Florio, John, 91; translator of Montaigne, 108.

Frobisher, Martin, Third Expedition of, 49; 78-79.

Golding, Arthur, 7; 15; 18.

Grays, Inn, 22-24.

Hackney, King's Place, family moves to, 104; sonnets found in, 137; 151; 153.

Hall, William, 151; 153.

Harington, Sir John chastised by Queen, 144; describes Queen's last days, 145.

Harvey, Gabriel, praise of Oxford, 38-39.

Hatton, Sir Christopher, 80.

Heminge and Condell, help with First Folio, 154.

Howard, Lord Henry, lie to Oxford, 45; converted Oxford to Catholicism, 51; sponsors Anne Vavasor, 52; plot against Queen, 55.

Jonson, Ben, dedicates First Folio, 155-160; writes of Droeshout engraving, 162-163.

King James I, 135; 147.

Lennox, Lady, 14.

Leicester, Earl of. See Dudley, Sir Robert.

Looney, J. T., identifies Oxford, 1-2.

Lyly, John, member of group, 6; secretary to Oxford, 6; 66-67; author of Euphues, 66; mentioned in letter of Oxford, 46; directs Paul's boys, 73; poem from Campaspe, 186.

Marlow, Christopher, in Oxford's group, 6; 65.

Meres, Francis, tribute to Oxford, 105; 150.

Montgomery, Philip Herbert, Earl of, married to Susan de Vere, 105; responsibility for First Folio, 153; Folio dedicated to him, 159; finances Folio, 160.

Munday, Anthony, member of Oxford group, 6; secretary to Oxford, 66-67; poem to Oxford, 186.

music, 68-69; Oxford's love of, 19.

Nashe, Thomas, member of Oxford's group, 66.

Norfolk, Duke of, aspires to marry Queen of Scots, 37-38; involved with Catholic faction, and death, 38.

Norris, Sir John, in command, Netherlands, 90.

Nowell, Laurence, 15-16; 18.

Oxford, Sixteenth Earl of, at Hedingham, 7; death, 11, sponsors actors' troupe, 70-71.

Oxford, Edward de Vere, Seventeenth Earl of, as author, 2-6; education, 12-25; lineage, 11; at Court, 16-17; troubles, 15-18; 37-38; 45-46; 55-56; 57; bears Sword of State, 29; 89-90; 101; at opening of Parliament, 29; relations with Queen, 32-34; marriage negotiations, 36-37; flight to Continent, 37; marriage to Anne Cecil, 37; involvement with Norfolk, 37-38; travels on Continent, 42-45; description in Chapman's play, 42-44; growing hostility to Burghley, 44-46; return to England, 45; antagonism to wife, 45-46; brings gloves for Queen, 48; invests in Frobisher Expedition, 49-50; tennis court quarrel, 50-51; converted to Catholicism, 51; affair with Anne Vavasor, 52-59; birth of son, 56; imprisonment in Tower, 56; duel with Sir Thomas Knyvvet, 57; break with mistress, 58; return to wife, 60; loyalty to Queen, 63-64; 125-126; judge at trial of Queen of Scots, 64; receives grant from Crown, 64; rival literary groups, 65; Oxford's group, 65-67; love of music, 68-69; death of wife, 69; actor, 103; maintains actors' troupe, 72-74; directions to actors, 74; love of his son, 81; return to Anne Vavasor, 82; sends son to Leyden, 85; Spanish Armada, 89; negotiates with Southampton as son-in-law, 91-99; *Venus and Adonis*, 94; *Lucrece*, 95; first printing of name, *Shake-speare*, 94; woos Elizabeth Trentham, 100; second marriage, 103; appears to retainer, 106; tribute to Burghley, 107; philosophy of, 107-108; presides at trial of Essex, 128-139; attends Queen last time, 140; at Queen's funeral, 147; at coronation of James, 147; death, 147.

Oxford, Seventeenth Earl of, Poems and Prose. *Loss of My Good Name*, 17-18; *Labour and its Reward*, 39-40; *Were I a King*, 51; *When I was Fair and Young*, 126; *Fancy and Desire*, 174; *Megliora Spero*, 175; *What Cunning Can Express*, 176; *With This There's a Red . . .* , 177; *Revenge of Wrong*, 180; *Anne Vavasor's Echo Song*, 181; *Love and Antagonism*, 177; *Love Thy Choice*, 187; *Woman's Changeableness*, 188; *Introduction to Cardanus' Comfort*, 170-171.

Oxford, Henry de Vere, Eighteenth Earl of, birth, 104; attains earldom, 147; responsibility for First Folio, 153.

Oxford's group, 6; 65-68.

Parliament, 29; 140.

Peele, George, in Oxford group, 65.

Pembroke, Mary Sidney, Countess of, in Oxford's group, 6, 66; invests in Third Frobisher Expedition, 50.

196

Pembroke, William Herbert, Earl of betrothed to Bridget de Vere, 105; responsibility for First Folio, 153; Folio dedicated to him, 159; finances First Folio, 160.

plays, History Plays, 65; reasons for anonymity, 77-78.

plays, *All's Well*, 5; *Antony and Cleo.*, 53; *As You Like It*, 155; *Coriolanus*, 131; *Hamlet*, 2; 3; 17; 45; 50; 74; 145; *Henry V*, 132; *Henry VI, Pt. I and II*, 65; *Julius Caesar*, 120; *King Lear*, 83, 108; *King Richard II*, 13, 22, 155; *Love's Labours Lost*, 77; *Macbeth*, 14; *Merchant of Venice*, 78, 98; *Merry Wives*, 124; *Midsummer Night's Dream*, 99; *Romeo and Juliet*, 37; *Troilus and Cressida*, 5; *Twelfth Night*, 68, 78.

portraits of Shakespeare, Holy Trinity bust, 162; Droeshout engraving, 162; Hampton Court, 164; Janssen, 165; Ashbourne, 165-167; revelations of X-rays, 163.

Puritans, 123-124.

Queen Elizabeth, at Hedingham, 7-10; at Cecil House, 14; royal progresses, 26; appearance at palace, 28-30; royal processions, London, 31; opening Parliament, 31; relations with Oxford, 32-34; rage at Oxford's disappearance, 41; permits travel, 41; receives gloves, 48; resumes affair, 48-49; jealousy of Anne Vavasor, 54; approves grant, 64; relations with Burghley, 110, 113, 114, 119; tribute from Burghley, 107; life story, 121-127; love affairs, 125; encouragement of drama, 123-124; handles Essex, 134; last appearance in Parliament, 140, 142; last days, 144-147; death and funeral, 147.

Queen Elizabeth's poems *I grieve*, 34, *When I was fair and young*. 126.

Roses, 13.

Sidney, Sir Philip, at Gray's Inn, 24; at Court, 50-51; invests in Frobisher Expedition, 50; tennis court quarrel, 50-51; poem to Oxford, 51; rival literary groups, 65; fighting in Netherlands, 90; death, 91.

Smith, Sir Thomas, 15-16, 111.

Sonnets, *1, 2*, 93; *3*, 94; *22*, 58; *26*, 86; *29*, 55; *36*, 84; *41*, 96; *44*, 86; *45*, 87; *57*, 53; *66*, 59; *67*, 84; *82*, 95; *87*, 98; *110*, 103; *112*, 102; *122*, 54; *125*, 101; *126*, 104; *137*, 58; *144*, 96; *152*, 82; referred to by Meres, 150; first collected edition, 153.

Southampton, Henry Wriothesley, Third Earl of, 91; marriage negotiations, 91-97; character, 92; attachment to Essex, 92; betrothal to Elizabeth de Vere, 91-97; marries Elizabeth Vernon, 97; implication in treachery, 136; trial, 136-139; imprisoned in Tower, 139; pardoned, 139.

Spenser, Sir Edmund, *Rosalind*, 53; *Tears of the Muses*, 77.

Trentham, Elizabeth, character, 101; marriage, 103; inherited wealth, 104; birth of son, 104; sells King's place, 151; coat of arms, 167.

Vavasor, Anne, appearance and character, 52-53; provokes Queen's jealousy, 54; birth of son, 56; imprisonment in Tower, 56; Oxford returns to, 82; poem to Oxford, 183-184.

Vere, Sir Francis, 5; arranges education for Oxford's son, 85-86; tomb, 85.